LESSER-KNOWN TAI CHI LINEAGES

Li, Wu, Sun, Xiong

An Anthology of Articles from the *Journal of Asian Martial Arts*
Compiled by Michael A. DeMarco, M.A.

Disclaimer
Please note that the authors and publisher of this book are not responsible in any manner whatsoever for any injury that may result from practicing the techniques and/or following the instructions given within. Since the physical activities described herein may be too strenuous in nature for some readers to engage in safely, it is essential that a physician be consulted prior to training.

All Rights Reserved
No part of this publication, including illustrations, may be reproduced or utilized in any form or by any means, electronic or mechanical, including photocopying, recording, or by any information storage and retrieval system (beyond that copying permitted by sections 107 and 108 of the US Copyright Law and except by reviewers for the public press), without written permission from Via Media Publishing Company.

Warning: Any unauthorized act in relation to a copyright work may result in both a civil claim for damages and criminal prosecution.

Copyright © 2016
by Via Media Publishing Company
941 Calle Mejia #822, Santa Fe, NM 87501 USA

All articles in this anthology were originally
published in the *Journal of Asian Martial Arts*, and
Asian Martial Arts: Constructive Thoughts & Practical Application.
Listed according to the table of contents for this anthology:

Wong, Y.M. (2005), Vol. 14 No. 2, pp. 44-51
Cai, N. (2006), Vol. 15 No 1, pp. 76-85
Burroughs, J. (2008), Vol. 17 No. 4, pp. 42-55
DeMarco, M. (2009), Vol. 18 No. 3, pp. 18-39

Book and cover design by
Via Media Publishing Company

Edited by Michael A. DeMarco, M.A.

Cover illustration
Defending against an attack from Anthony Natale,
Jake Burroughs utilizes a technique from the Sun Taiji system
Photograph courtesy of: www.groundnevermisses.com

ISBN: 978-1893765382

www.viamediapublishing.com

contents

iv **Preface**
by Michael DeMarco, M.A.

CHAPTERS

1 **From a Small Village to the Capital:
The Li Family's Early Taijiquan Curriculum**
by Wong Yuenming

11 **In Memory of Wu Daxin: Wu Family Taiji Boxing Gatekeeper**
by Cai Naibiao; Y. L. Yip and Leroy Clark, Trans.

22 **A Comprehensive Introduction to
Sun Family Taiji Boxing Theory and Applications**
by Jake Burroughs, B.A.

42 **Xiong Style Taiji in Taiwan: Historical Development
& a Photographic Expose Featuring Master Lin Jianhong**
by Michael A. DeMarco, M.A.

70 **Index**

preface

Anyone who has studied taiji long enough to gain proficiency in the fundamental practices, probably has read enough to also grasp the general history and theory of the art. What we read influences our ideas about what the word "taiji" represents as a practice. For this reason, it is beneficial to look outside the mainstream writings to gain a broader view of the rich tradition taiji encompasses. A look at some of the lesser-known lineages can illustrate fascets of taiji that would have otherwise been overlooked or under appreciated.

In the first chapter in this anthology, Wong Yuenming details the Li Family Taiji style as it developed from the teachings of Yang Luchan. Sources state that Yang Luchan gave his student Wang Lanting classics writings from Yang's teacher Chen Changxing, manuals, secret instructions, "heart transmissions," and various notes. Wang's gifted disciple, Li Ruidong, formulated a curriculum that was uniquely immense, including training regimens he inherited at the turn of the century.

Cai Naibiao's chapter focuses on a "gatekeeper" of Wu Family Style Taijiquan, Wu Daxin. He was the grandson of Wu Jianquan (1870-1942), the founder of this lineage. Daxin was particularly famous for his taiji saber skills. The author is a lineage holder living in Hong Kong and was able to provide much information and insights into the life and contributions of Wu Daxin.

Training in Sun Lutang's taiji style presents not only an extremely healthy exercise, but also an effective system of combat as author Jake Burroughs discusses in chapter three. This is a concise yet inclusive overview of Sun Family Taiji boxing, including the historical background, real-world applications, and the theory involved in this often overlooked system of taiji. Burroughs is assisted in photographic presentations by Tim Cartmell.

The final chapter presents a branch of Yang Style as taught by Xiong Yanghe (1888-1981), who was a leading scholar/practitioner in Taiwan over the decades. Information assembled here provides a comprehensive overview of Xiong Style Taiji. Included are Xiong's lineage, his preservation of the system, and its significance for the understanding taijiquan as a martial art and exercise for health.

Michael A. DeMarco, Publisher
Santa Fe, New Mexico
October 2016

chapter 1

From a Small Village to the Capital:
The Li Family's Early Taijiquan Curriculum

by Wong Yuen Ming

Chinese characters for Li Family School.
Zhang Shaotang (b. 1952), fourth generation Li Style master practicing.
All illustrations courtesy of Wong Yuen Ming.

Introduction

Hebei Province in northern China has been home to number of notable martial artists in the last couple hundred years. Placing their capital in Beijing, the Qing Dynasty attracted many accomplished teachers who were looking for fortune, some found careers as escorts for the many rich merchants traveling across the country, and many others as martial arts teachers. The most influential taijiquan figure of that period was without doubt Yang Luchan (1799-c. 1875), who reached Beijing around 1850 with plenty of experience gained from numerous trips to Chen Village (birthplace of Chen Family Style Taiji). Later on, he taught in his hometown of Yongnian. Modern taijiquan history basically started with Yang's arrival in the capital, and especially with his appointment to the court.

Yang Luchan Goes to Beijing

Yang Luchan went to Beijing with an introduction from Wu Ruqing[1] to teach at a rich family's compound. Wu Tunan (?-1988)[2] explains how Ruqing, who had passed the imperial examinations and was appointed to Beijing, had a friend called Mr. Zhang. Zhang's brother loved martial arts and, having heard about Yang Luchan from Ruqing, invite Yang to the family estate to teach (Ma,

1984). In a short time, Yang and his two sons were working at the Zhang mansion training the young Zhang Fengqi.

According to Wu Tunan's account, the Zhangs had a successful preserved vegetable business and one of their outlets was in Xiang Shan, very close to where Prince Zaiyi[3] used to hunt. According to this story, Prince Zaiyi often stopped over at the Zhang's on the way back to the palace to purchase some of their famous preserved vegetables. On one of these visits, the prince happened to see Yang Luchan training Zhang Fengqi. Luchan's skills intrigued the prince, who invited him to his estate. This anecdote notes that the Zhangs were not happy with this at first, so an arrangement was made allowing Yang to teach at the prince's residence the first two weeks of the month, and continue his teaching at the Zhang's the second half of each month.

However, the Li family has a slightly different story.[4] Wang Lanting (1829-?) wrote in 1874 that his introduction to the art of taijiquan was in the fourth year of the Tongzhi Era (1865) through his colleague Fu Zhongquan,[5] a military guard who worked at the Dun Prince Residence.[6] Three years later when Wang was promoted to chief officer (a third grade officer),[7] he had the chance to spend some time again with Fu Zhongquan. Realizing taijiquan's depth, Wang decided to follow Fu to Dongzhi Men, an area in Beijing where Yang Luchan was teaching. After encountering Yang, Wang asked to be accepted as disciple and later offered Yang a teaching position at the Dun Prince Residence.

Yang was in charge of training the guards, who were mainly of Manchu heritage and already quite skilled in martial arts. The most famous of this group were the three comrades Wu Quanyou (1834-1902),[8] Ling Shan, and Wan Chun. All later studied under Yang Banhou (1837-1892, second son of Yang Luchan), and are therefore referred as third generation students in most Yang family writings. Contrary to common knowledge, Yang Luchan accepted a number of disciples most of whom were only vaguely mentioned in later Yang literature, which focused mainly on his direct family successors. Some of these earlier students were completely written out of the Yang lineage by the second generation upon failing to accept the tutelage of Yang Banhou after Yang Luchan's death.

Wang Lanting's original name was Yongtai. He remained under Yang Luchan's tutelage for seven years, until Yang's death. This may sound odd to the general reader who believes Yang Luchan died in 1872. A brief explanation is necessary to put this information into perspective.

According to written and oral sources that Wang Lanting passed on to his disciple Li Ruidong (1851-1917), Yang Luchan died in Beijing between 1875 and 1880. Yang gave Wang a complete set of literature, which included classics (*jingpu*) from Yang Luchan's teacher Chen Changxing, manuals (*zongpu*), secret instructions (*koujue*), "heart transmissions" (*xinfa*), and various notes. Wang Lanting's manual preface dated 1874 specifies that Wang "was accepted as a disciple in the seventh year of the Tongzhi Era (1868) … and studied for seven years," not mentioning the death of Yang, thus confirming he was still alive when the preface was written. Later, Li Ruidong corroborates this assumption in his preface adding that "the old Master [Yang Luchan] died at the beginning of the Guangxu Era [starting 1875] … [A]t the beginning of the Guangxu Era, I received the true transmission of taijiquan from my senior [*shixiong*] Wang Lanting.…" This preface notes that, on behalf of Yang who had just died, Wang Lanting passed his knowledge to Li Ruidong. Since Wang and Li first met at the Li's residence in the fourth month of the sixth year of the Guangxu Era (1880), we are left with the first six years of Guangxu (1875 to 1880).

These manuals were then passed down to Li Ruidong, who added his insights along with manuals from his other teachers. The body of his transmission was originally called the Li Style martial system. It was later renamed Wuqing Taijiquan in respect of Master Li's birthplace and because of his emphasis on taiji. In the last 20 years or so, his descendants have started to refer to the school as Li Taijiquan in an attempt to standardize its name with the common custom of naming family styles with the family name.

Great Master Li Ruidong

Li Ruidong (aka, Li Shuxun) was born in 1851 in Wuqing Prefecture (Tianjin) to a very rich and influential family. His father, Li Xiaoji, was a famous doctor and owned a medicine business. Their mansion had over eighty guestrooms, which people of skills in various arts visited all year round. The young Li Ruidong was attracted to martial arts since childhood, and his father, having seen his inclinations, arranged for various masters to teach his son and personally taught him traditional Chinese medicine.

Left: Li Ruidong (b. 1851), founder of Li Style Taijiquan.
Right: Li Jiying, third son of Li Ruidong.

In 1880, the chief of the Dun Prince Palace guards, Wang Lanting, was passing by Wuqing and briefly visited his acquaintance, Li Xiaoji. The first night during dinner, Li Ruidong started to ask Wang about his favorite subject, martial arts. Lanting explained that he used to study Twelve Continuous Fists (*Shier Lianquan*, a branch of *xinyiquan*) but that he had switched to taijiquan after meeting Master Yang Luchan and had been learning from Dong Haichuan (1804-1880, founder of *baguazhang*) after his teacher passed away. Li Ruidong asked to continue the discussion in the library, were the two moved to drink some tea.

Having heard of the Yang family, Li asked Wang if he knew of Yang Banhou. Lanting replied, "He is not a stranger, of course. He is my junior classmate and son of my late teacher." In hearing this, Li got excited and asked if he could test his skills against Master Wang. With each of three attacks, Li Ruidong was sent to the floor. Impressed with such martial ability, Li immediately asked to be accepted as a disciple. Wang replied that, given his relationship with Li's father, he considered Li a junior of the same generation and was going to teach him on behalf of Master Yang. Wang Lanting proposed Li follow him to the capital, where he was first offered the position of officer of Garden Management (a fifth grade officer), which was mainly a seasonal job where he could have plenty of time to practice with Wang.

Zhang Wansheng,
third generation Li Style master.

Early Curriculum and Learning Progression

In the preface by Li Ruidong dated 1881 of the family taijiquan manual, he recounts this learning progression:

> I first studied 13 postures, then I learned the 64 forms, and I was given a manual that was a must read for beginners.... I studied eight positions, five steps, and eight techniques, all at the various levels of solo practice, partner practice, solo stepping, partner stepping, solo exercise, partner exercise, solo killing, partner killing....

We can see here the original progression of study passed down to Li Ruidong. Later in the manual, the complete list of movements and description of those forms are recorded. Needless to say, Li was not a beginner, but we can establish from the same source that the above material was transmitted over three years. The 64 sequence is also referred to as the "Henan 64 Form," and it was possibly developed in Henan by the Chen family on the foundation of the earlier 13 postures, although its description and appearance do not entirely fit into modern Chen style.

This material has been handed down from Yang Luchan to Wang Lanting, from Wang to Li, and is still part of Li curriculum. It is important to note the approach to training even more than the curriculum itself. Every movement is studied and performed alone many times. After many repetitions, the movement is held in a standing practice before going on with a new set. As for all other exercises, the progression for practice is from beginner practice to solo practice to partner practice.

Li Ruidong explains in his "Four Important Points of Solo Practice":

> *Danlian* is solo practice. While practicing alone, we do not have to strive [to subdue an opponent] but only try to get familiar [with the exercise]. We can choose one or two exercises and practice them—this is called learning appearance. We can take three or five exercises and perform them without rest—this is called learning breath. We can take a few simple moves and practice them at will—this is called learning the law. Or we can practice as per our imagination—this is called learning the secret wisdom. Taken together, these are the Four Important Points of Solo Practice....

> The law creates the appearance, the appearance moves the breath, borrowing the breath gives birth to the secret wisdom, acting the secret wisdom leads to the law...

> Without practicing the appearance, the appearance is not firm. Without practicing the breath, the breath is not smooth. Without practicing the secret wisdom, the secret wisdom is not active. Without practicing the

law, the law does not break through. There is a progression and if one does not understand the law and wastes his time practicing the appearance, the appearance is not true. Trying to practice the secret wisdom without practicing the breath, the secret wisdom is not alive. Trying to practice the law without practicing the secret wisdom, the law is not round....

It was therefore the "eight doors" with the "five steps" that formed the curriculum's foundation. They were practiced first according to the beginner procedure (*chulian*), learning one movement at a time and holding it in the stillness of standing meditation and following the solo practice sequence. Only later were they linked to form the 13 postures and the 64 forms. The eight forms, with the foundation of five steps, then generate the eight techniques/energies (*peng, lu, ji, an, cai, lie, zhou, kao*) that were performed at that time in both large and small frames.

After having progressed in solo practice, there was an intermediary phase in which the student receives from the teacher the oral explanations of the "five secrets" along with the practical "adjustment of hands and eyes." This is extremely important, but not easily covered within a few words and would be better addressed in a future writing.

The next step was partner practice, the door to practical employment of one's skill to combat. Li Ruidong passed down a "Three Important Points on Partner Practice":

> *Shuanglian* means practicing with a partner. When practicing with a partner, one should not follow a preset form, doing a preset form becomes a dead system. Those who practice this way abandon their hearts and rush with their spirit, hands and feet execute false movements. They bend, but do not reach out, just like a theater performance showing an empty form, like a story without heart—only a nice looking picture for the pleasure of those watching. Practicing like this for long does not only lead to no accomplishment, but it is also dangerous. If one wants to get benefit from partner practice, it is essential to receive constant instructions from a skilled teacher.
>
> With a practice companion, one carries an attack and one defends in order to train the distance and investigate each other's movement, thus understanding the principles of change. These are the two first important points. Then each partner chooses his favorite techniques and apply them full-force in order to learn the importance of applications.
>
> Taken altogether, these are the Three Important Points.

Basically, within this framework of training, the introduction to actual fighting was a period of attack/response in which the apprentice was supposed to learn timing, distance, and the principles of change behind each movement. Once these points were understood, it was basically free fighting, where the students were expected to test their embodiment of the principles of the eight gates (*bamen*) and five steps (*wubu*) and react accordingly.

The reader may have noticed that no mention of "push hands" was made. I believe push hands was especially popular among descendants of Yang Luchan as a useful tool for friendly reciprocal test of skills when true fighting was not necessary. However, push hands has gained much significance and broader acceptance since it was introduced, although seldom practiced, by the 2nd and 3rd generations of the Li family. They practice this mainly to meet the expectations of outsiders who are looking at a polite reciprocal test of skills. Most teachers in this lineage are quick to remind students that friendly and methodic exchanges like those in push hands easily get the practitioner to fall into a "dead system" that Li Ruidong warned about.

Li Ruidong had few equals during his time. His curriculum was immense, including training regimens he inherited from some of the most gifted martial artists at the turn of the century, which we will investigate later.

Useful Definitions

13 postures: referred to as the early taijiquan routine based on the combination of the 8 doors and the 5 steps.

8 doors (*bamen*): sometimes referred as the 8 techniques (see below).

8 techniques: 8 expressions of fundamental taijiquan energies/movements—wardoff (*peng*), rollback (*lu*), press (*ji*), push (*an*), pluck (*cai*), split (*lie*), elbow (*zhou*), and bump (*kao*).

8 forms (*bashi*): set of exercises based on the 8 doors.

5 steps (*wubu*): 5 main spatial directions giving form to taijiquan footwork.

64 forms: enlarged version of the earlier 13 postures, possibly created at the Chen village and passed down to Yang Luchan.

Large and small frames: the two main approaches to practice, in particular referring to their relative external appearance, being compact or expanded.

Li Family Lineage

Li Ruidong

- Li Boying (1894-1951) son
  - Cao Zhenhan
  - Liu Jianqing
- Li Zhongying (1896-1921) son
  - Fang Zhixuan
- Li Jiying (1901-1961) son
  - Zheng Binzhang
- Li Qiying (1892-1960) daughter
  - Yang Guifu
- Li Juying (1898-1958) daughter
  - Li Xing
    - Zhang Shaotang (1952-)
  - Zhang Zhaolai
    - Jia Shiwen
- Wang Fengming
- Xiang Runtian (1854-1942)
  - Zhang Wansheng (1932-1992)
    - Qin Xilin
- Liu Ziming
    - Wang Qinghe
- Chen Jixian (1883-1960)
  - Hao Ming
    - Zhou Hong
- Li Zilian (1866-1948)
  - Du Xiansan
    - Xu Guoliang
- Zhang Tao (1865-1941)
  - Li Zongwen
- Li Jinxiu (1858-1938)
  - Li Zongwu
- Gao Ruizhou
- Chen Chijie
- Luo Ziming
  - Chen Yuefang
- Jiang Wanliang
  - Ren Wanliang
- Jiang Wanhe
  - Han Laiyu
- He Xueli
- Sun Jinchen
  - Li Zhaotang
- Wen Shiquan
  - Li Zhaodi
- Monk Chen An
  - Li Zhaoyin
- Wang Run
  - Wang Bin

Glossary

Ba dashi	八大勢	Shidi	師弟
Ba xiaoshi	八小勢	Shier lianquan	十二連拳
Bafa	八法	Shijing	試勁
Baobiao	保標	Shixiong	師兄
Bashi	八勢	Shuangcao	雙操
Chenjiakou	陳家溝	Shuanglian	雙練
Chulian	初練	Shuanglian sanyao	雙練三要
Dancao	單操	Shuangsha	雙殺
Danlian	單練	Shuangxing	雙行
Danlian siyao	單練四要	Sifa	死法
Dansha	單殺	Taiji shisan shi	太極十三勢
Danxing	單行	Tianjin	天津
Dong Haichuan	董海川	Tongzhi (era)	同治
Dongzhi Men	東直門	Tuishou	推手
Fu Zhongquan	富仲權	Wan Chun	萬春
Guangxu (era)	光緒	Wang Lanting (Yongtai)	王蘭亭 (永泰)
Henan style 64 form	河北六十四勢	Wu Ruqing	武汝清
Ji	機	Wu Tunan	吳圖南
Jingpu	經譜	Wu Yuxiang	武禹襄
Koujue	口訣	Wubu	五步
Li	理	Wujing	武清
Li Ruidong (Shuxun)	李瑞東 (樹勛)	Wujue	五決
Li Xiaoqi	李小歧	Xiang Shan	香山
Ling Shan	凌善 (山)	Xinfa	心法
Lipai Quanfa	李派拳法	Xinyiquan	心意拳
Prince Duan	端王	Yang Banhou	楊班侯
Prince Dun	惇王	Yang Luchan	楊露蟬
Prince Zaiyi	載漪	Yongnian	永年
Qi	氣	Zhang Fengqi	張鳳岐
Quanpu	拳譜	Zhanzhuang	站樁
Quanyou (Wu)	全佑	Zongpu	宗譜
Shi	勢		

Notes

1. Elder brother of the more famous Wu Yuxiang, who was an early disciple of Yang Luchan in their hometown of Yongnian and whose descendants later originated the Wu/Hao style.
2. Famous taijiquan teacher and scholar, disciple of Wu Jianquan (1870-1941).
3. Prince Zaiyi was the birth name of Prince Duan.
4. When Yang Luchan got to the prince's residence in 1868, Zaiyi was only thirteen. Zaiyi got married in 1885, and was ennobled as Prince Duan in 1889.
5. It is very probable that Fu Zhongquan was none other than Fu Zhou, whose descendants teach mainly in Baoding what they call "Inside the Palace Taijiquan" (*Funei Pai Taijiquan*).
6. Fifth son of the Daoguan Emperor (r. 1821-1850) and father of Prince Duan.
7. Officers were divided into nine grades with additional subcategories to create the so-called "Nine Grades, Eighteen Levels."
8. His son Wu Jianquan then used the surname Wu to create the name Wu Style Taijiquan.
9. In traditional Chinese society, family bonds and roles are quite strict. The same applies to martial arts families, two students from the same generation would refer to themselves as to "elder brother" and "younger brother." In certain schools, this refers to the amount of time in practice as opposed to actual age.

Bibliography

Li Family. (1874). *Taijiquan family manual*. Unpublished manuscript. Wang Lanting's preface dated 1874. Li Ruidong's preface dated 1881.

Ma Y.Q. (Ed.). (1984). *Research on Taijiquan*. Hong Kong: Commercial Press.

chapter 2

In Memory of Wu Daxin:
Wu Family Taiji Boxing Gatekeeper

by Cai Naibiao; Translated by Y. L. Yip and Leroy Clark

Wu Daxin on his birthday in 2005.
Newspaper advertisement dated July 14, 2001: an announcement stating that
Wu Daxin formally takes up post of gatekeeper of the Wu Style lineage.

On January 16, 2005, Wu Daxin (Wu Tai-sin; cant. Ng Dai Sun) passed away quietly at the Hong Kong Sanatorium Hospital. Wu was the latest in the bloodline of Wu family style taijiquan adepts, representing the 4th generation and selected as "gatekeeper" of the family boxing art. The gatekeeper is the main person who represents, guards, and monitors the family art. This person is selected and appointed by the previous gatekeeper, usually a blood relative. The person selected must have attained a respectable skill level, appropriate knowledge, and a suitable personality to represent the family system.

Wu Daxin was born in Mainland China on November 26th, 1933, only 22 years after the fall of the Qing Dynasty (1644-1911). It was an era of warlords, civil strife, and war. It was also the period immediately preceding the invasion and horrific occupation by Japan. Wu Daxin's father was Wu Gongzao (1903-1983), the second son of Wu Jianquan (1870-1942), and younger brother of Wu Gongyi (1900-1970). He was the brother of Wu Daxin.

In the mid-1930's, the Wu family was forced to move from Shanghai in order to avoid the unrest and warfare in China. In doing so, the family passed through Guangzhou, Macao, and finally settled in Hong Kong. Their sole means of support was their family heritage, i.e., the martial art of taiji boxing.

The family managed to survive and eventually thrive in such a poor, small island town because it had already secured fame in taiji boxing throughout China. By the time the Wu's had settled in Hong Kong, there were many rich celebrities, traveled and educated merchants, and societal movers and shakers in Hong Kong and Macao who knew of the Wu's boxing art. The family established a foothold on Hennessy Road in Wanchai, a Hong Kong suburb.

This Hong Kong neighborhood was home to the red light bar district described famously in the 1960 movie, "The World of Suzie Wong." The area later became the proving grounds for Wu Dakui's (1923-1972) taiji skills. He was the eldest son of Gongyi and eldest grandson of Wu Jianquan. Dakui fought and defeated dozens of porters and workers on the rough waterfront. He was undefeated in Wanchai and before that on the Pearl River Delta, where Hong Kong, Macao, Guangzhou, Fo Shan, and Shun De are found. The area was a virtual gold mine of martial artists. This was the home of the famous Huang Feihong (cant. Wong Fei Hung, 1847-1924) and Ye Wen (cant. Yip Man, 1893-1972); and also the home of Li Haiquan (cant. Lee Hoi Chuen, 1901-1965, father of Bruce Lee).

Wanchai District at night.

The Wu family was later invited to teach taiji for the Hong Kong Jin Wu Sports Association, South China Sports Association, and the Hong Kong YMCA. These teaching endeavors, however, lasted only a few years. By 1941, Hong Kong had fallen to the Japanese military. Refusing to be exploited by the invaders, the patriotic Wu family fled in several small groups back to Shanghai. Not until 1945, with Japan's surrender, did the Wu family return to Hong Kong.

This author was also born on Mainland China. By 1932, my mother brought my family to Hong Kong to avoid the war, civil strife, and the debilitating famine. I remember suffering through the infamous, meager food rationing of that war period. After the war, I entered the Jianquan Taiji Association on Lockhart Road in Wanchai and studied Wu's boxing method.

In the beginning, Zhong Yueping[1] taught me. He later became my "gongfu elder brother" (*shixiong*). It was at that time that I met the young Daxin. I knew immediately that he had suffered nearly the same fate as I had. His parents were far away on Mainland China because of the war. The only difference was that I was an orphan by that time. We became the closest of friends. On weekends, we used to go to Shatin in the New Territories to Shen Xianglin's villa. Shen was a senior disciple of Gongyi. Daxin and I slept in the same room. In fact, this was where Shen and his sons, Shen Dongqiang and Shen Dongfu, and Shen's godson, "Rock" Wu Guotai, studied under Gongyi on weekends.

Even as late as 1997, during the handover of the British Colony, I was asked by then gatekeeper Wu Yanxia (1930-2001) to share the teaching load a few nights a week with Daxin in the Jordan School. Sometimes he would arrive early in the afternoon. He would then plead with me to accompany him to various places in the city, sometimes as far away as Yuan Lang, near the Chinese border. We visited restaurants to snack on to pass away the time. Daxin shared some of his food with me while waiting there.

Master Wu Daxin followed his uncle Wu Gongyi in taiji boxing up to his uncle's 1972 death. Daxin was always at his master's side throughout the day as well as when the master taught boxing. He was like a son to him. Gongyi said that Daxin was the one who had learned the most from him and the one who received most of his art. "As for how much he eventually achieves," Gongyi also said, "it depends strictly on his diligence."

This was quite unlike Gongyi's own two sons. Wu Jianquan raised and taught taiji to Gongyi's oldest son, Dakui. Wu Gongyi's younger son, Daqi (1926-1993), was absent for many years while his father was still alive, having gone to Southeast Asia to teach taiji.

During the mid-1950's, after I had finished assisting Zhong Yueping teach on the top floor of the Lockhart Road school, we would go down one flight of stairs to the fourth floor where the main school was located.[2] Shortly after that, Wu Gongyi began to teach advanced material to Daxin, Zhong Yueping, and Guo Shaojiong, husband of Wu Yanxia. As a junior, I was only allowed to observe from the sideline. After those sessions, we would invite Gongyi to a restaurant for a late night snack. Those were memorable days indeed. This was also how Daxin received so much personal coaching from Wu Gongyi.

There are some very special events about Daxin I remember with fondness and with awe. Around 1954 or 1955, one night after the annual celebration of the birthday of Daoist Grandmaster Zhang Sanfeng, we were in the Kam Ling (man. Jinling) Restaurant. The dinner party had finished. We left the restaurant and walked down the street only to find that gang members had punctured Wu Dakui's car tires. The street thugs were standing brazenly nearby. A brawl broke out and Daxin was grabbed from behind and attacked by three of the hoodlums. In one single motion, he punched the two in front and freed himself from the bear hug. All three fell down. They immediately scrambled up and ran away.

Left: The author and Wu Daxin (r.) on a liner heading for Singapore on June 29, 1956.
Right: left to right: Liao Xiangsang (cant. Lau Heung Sang), Cai Naibiao, Wu Gongzao (1903-1983), Wu Dazhun, and Wu Kangnian (cant. Ng Hong Nin). Photograph taken in Shanghai, outside the Jianquan Taiji Association's Main School, June 12, 1981.

I remember well the date January 17th, 1954, when twenty-year old Daxin along with Zhong Yueping were the two personal assistants to Wu Gongyi for the famous Wu-Chan fight.[3] They assisted in the ring as well as on the trip from Hong Kong to Macao and back again.

On June 29th, 1956, Daxin took the Liner Carthage to Singapore to take the reins of the Jianquan Taiji Association there. This was really a milestone in Wu Family Taiji development because of the influence he would have there.

In 1979, Wu Gongzao, Daxin's father and the younger son of Jianquan, came to Hong Kong. The family was at last reunited after a separation of many years. Wu Gongzao mostly taught the most senior students such as Zhong Yueping and Lu Botang.

The book *Wu Family Taijiquan* (known as the *Gold Book*; Wu, 1984), based on Gongzao's taijiquan (known as the *Green Book*, 1933) was published in Hong Kong. Many observed that Gongzao's leg had been traumatized.[4] After some time, Gongzao gradually recovered. His fundamentals were still very impressive. He was much better than us even at his advanced age and in his poor physical condition. We could push and attack with all our might, yet he did not shift his step even one bit. His style looked similar to that of his nephew, Wu Dakui. But then, they had both learned from father and grandfather Wu Jianquan. In 1982, he returned to Hunan to visit old friends. Unfortunately, he died there.

During his stay in Hong Kong, Gongzao tried to arrange a marriage for Daxin. He wrote me about it. He told us his old injury, caused by the decades of confinement and torture, had been cured by a lady with excellent acupuncture skills. I had been present during some of those treatment sessions. It really was quite remarkable. After some massage and the removal of the inserted acupuncture needle, some old dark blood was extracted. Gongzao then felt much better. He was eventually cured. Gongzao was very grateful. He felt that the acupuncturist was an especially good person. He tried to arrange a marriage between her and his forty-year old son Daxin. It was unsuccessful and Daxin remained single. I have treasured this letter from Gongzao all these years because it is in Gongzao's valuable, personal handwriting. It is also a piece of Wu family history. In addition, it is a record of certain wonderful and amazing traditional medicine.

Left to right: Ma Jiangxiong (son of Ma Yueliang), Wu Gongzao (1903-1983), Wu Daizhung (cant. Ng TaiJing, elder brother of Wu Daxin), Wu Yinghua (1907-1997), and Ma Yueliang (1902-1998). Photograph taken in Jade Buddha Temple, Shanghai, 1981.

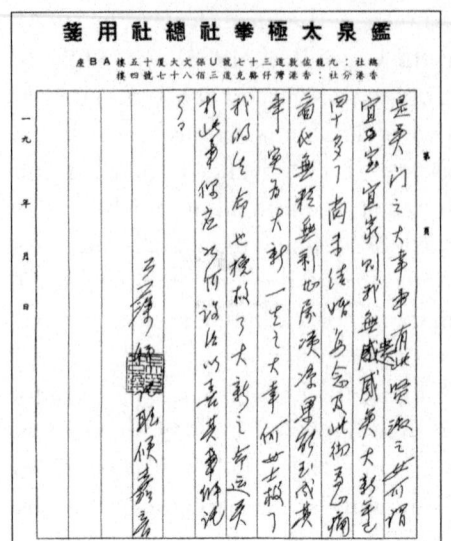

Handwritten letter from Wu Gongzao to Cai Naibiao which discusses introducing Wu Daxin to an acupuncturist who cured him. Dated 1982.

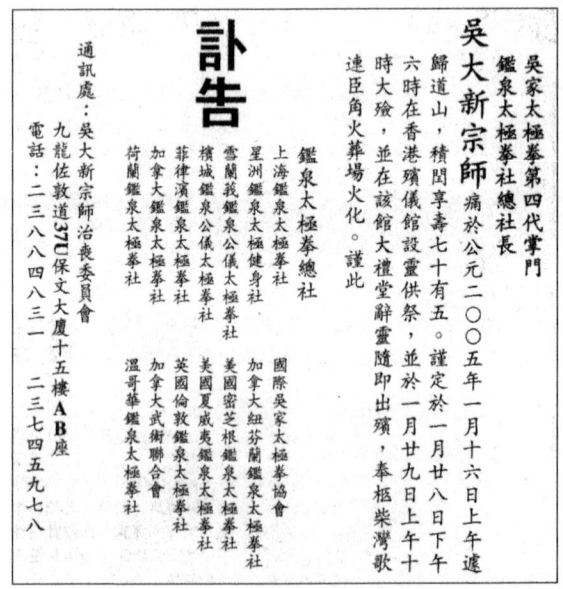

Newspaper obituary for Wu Daxin dated January 16, 2005.

In October 1988, the building holding the Lockhart Road School was to be demolished. Daxin purchased property on Moreton Terrace in Causeway Bay with his own funds.

After the 14 July 2001 death of Wu Yanxia, Daxin became the Wu family gatekeeper. The ceremony was held the next day in the Jordan Main School. A dinner party was held in the Best Seafood Restaurant (Ting Ho Restaurant) in the Tsim Sha Tsui section of Kowloon.

The first Wu family gatekeeper was Wu Quanyou, followed by his son, Wu Jianquan, then his son Wu Gongyi. After Gongyi's death, his son Wu Dakui became the gatekeeper in Hong Kong and outside China. Dakui died in 1972. His younger brother, Daqi, was then appointed gatekeeper. When Daqi passed away, the younger sister of Dakui and Daqi, Wu Yanxia, took over. She died in 2001. The above were all descendents of the Wu Gongyi line. Wu Daxin, on the other hand, was the son of Wu Jianquan's other son, Gongzao.

Master Daxin adopted ten batches of disciples; many are overseas. Among them are Wu Wenbiao, now chief coach in the Jordan Main School; Wu Kangnian, Wu Chaojie, Deng Huijian, and Kelvin Steel. Daxin and Wu Gongzao were famed for their taiji saber. Wu Gongyi, Wu Dakui, and Wu Yanxia were all very good with the double-edged sword. It is noteworthy that all of Wu's sword experts came from the Gongyi lineage. This had a direct effect on the disciples and was seen in their respective emphasis.

Daxin used to perform the saber routine during the annual Zhang Sanfeng Birthday Festival. In recent times, however, during Yanxia's term as gatekeeper, he also demonstrated push-hand exercises. Sometimes he would have his disciples demonstrate and then he would come out and teach them how they might improve. Once in a while he would demonstrate his simple, concise, and elegant solution to a particular situation. His skills were documented on video.

Wu Daxin and the author push-hands during celebrations for the annual Zheng Sanfeng (legendary founder of taijiquan) Birthday festival. Photographs taken in the Pearl City Restaurant, 1983 and 1984.

Daxin's push-hands skill was quite unique. More than any other, he really had the feel for Wu Gongyi's method. Seldom did he do push-hands in the school. Rather, he would just sit and observe. We frequently commented that Daxin seldom even moved his hands. Even when he did the exercise, he usually finished it off quickly with minimal moves.

Whenever I did push-hands with him, I would usually advance my hand and he would nearly simultaneously, directly strike back. It appeared he was attacking an attack. In fact, it was the advice of the ancients to wait until the other moves, but you arrive first. He did this in one simple coordinated movement. In fact, just his initial, interceptive position already nullified part of my attack. The strike on contact used a certain rotation and countered my offense. Thus he could just spiral back and nullify and borrow my energy. Outwardly, that movement looked plain and simple. However, it was anything but plain and simple. Those who tasted it were filled with awe and respect. The higher their level, the more appreciation students voiced. For this reason many followed him for years hoping just to see him show the movement. It was beautiful in its simplicity yet few could do it.

During a meeting of our generation with Master Daxin, sitting next to him were Lu Botang, my gongfu older brother (*shidai*) who used to be the "demonstration dummy" for Wu Gongyi, and who had written extensively about Wu Gongyi in the newspapers; and Ye Shuliang, the chief coach of the now-closed Wu Dakui Mongkok School. Ye used to collect the special tuition fee for Daxin when he taught saber in Dakui's school. Thus they were quite friendly with each other.

Left to right: Cai Naibiao with Xiao Huilong (cant. Siu Wai Lung) and Wu Daxin. Photograph taken in a Hong Kong restaurant on November 16, 2001, during a gathering to celebrate Wu Daxin's birthday. Mr. Xiao is the last surviving disciple who studied directly under Wu Jianquan.

Lu Botang asked about the progress Daxin had made over the years. Daxin just let the seated Lu grasp his wrist. Quite quickly, he made a slight imperceptible movement. Involuntarily, Lu stood up gently. Lu was totally bewildered as to how Daxin had done that. Daxin told them, "This is ward-off [peng]!" After this, Lu was completely convinced Daxin had indeed acquired Gongyi's art.

After this demonstration, Ye Shuliang asked Daxin for any special gems he might give them to further their practice. Daxin then uttered, "jing"— meaning silence, serenity. This was probably the last gem of wisdom he left us.

South China Morning Post newspaper reporter Ravina Shamdasani interviewed Daxin for an article when he was sixty-eight years old. It was the commemoration on becoming gatekeeper. Commenting on that and on his and his cousins' practice, Daxin said, "I was lazy practicing taiji when I was growing up." Others, however, remember him practicing very diligently and that he understood the family tradition had continued for generations. He said, "It is my duty and honor to carry the tradition forward." Daxin explained, "It is a heavy burden but we have been prepared from early childhood. In fact," he continued, "since I was in my mother's tummy." Wu Daxin was a superb master and gatekeeper.

Wu Style Taijiquan Lineage

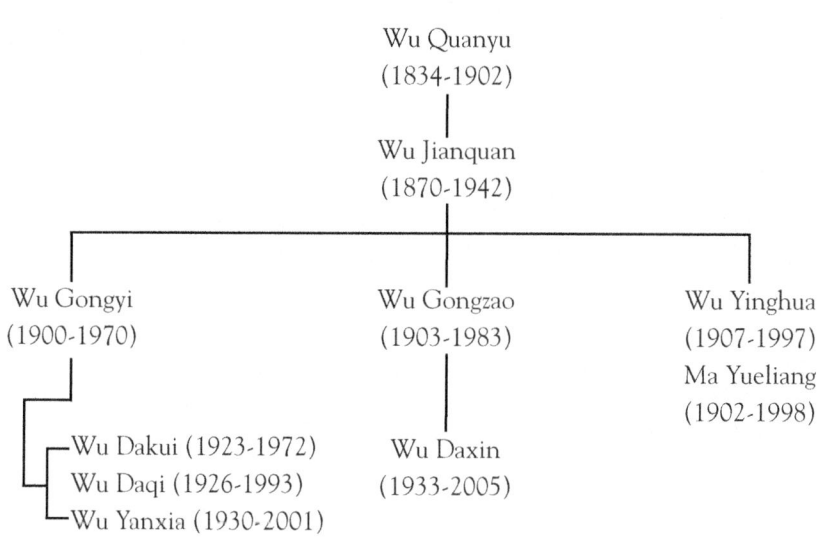

GLOSSARY

Pinyin		Cantonese (Hong Kong)
Cai Naibiao	蔡乃標	Tsoi Nie Biu
Deng Huijian	鄧惠堅	Dang Wai Gin
Fo Shan	佛山	Faat Shan
Guo Shaojiong	郭少炯	Kwok Siu Gwing
Huang Feihong	黃飛鴻	Wong Fei Hung
Jing	靜	Jing
Jian Quan	鑑泉	Kam Chuen
Taijiquan Association	太極拳社	Tai Chi Chuan Association
Li Haiquan	李海泉	Lee Hoi Chuen
Lu Botang	盧柏堂	Lo Pak Tong
Ma Yueliang	馬岳樑	Ma Ngok Leung
Shen Dongfu	沈東福	Shum Tung Fuk
Shen Dongqiang	沈東強	Shum Tung Keung
Shen Xianglin	沈香林	Shum Heung Lam
Shi Bo	師伯	Si Pak
Shi Di	師第	Si Tai
Shi Shu	師叔	Si Suk
Shi Xiong	師兄	Si Hing
Shun De	順德	Shun Tak
Wu Chaojie	吳超杰	Ng Chiu Kit
Wu Dakui	吳大揆	Ng Tai Kwai
Wu Daqi	吳大齊	Ng Tai Chai
Wu Daxin	吳大新	Ng Dai Sun
Wu Dazhun	吳大諄	Ng Tai Jeun
Wu Gongyi	吳公儀	Ng Kung Yee
Wu Gongzao	吳公藻	Ng Kung Cho
Wu Guotai	吳國泰	Ng Kwok Tai
Wu Jianquan	吳鑑泉	Ng Kam Chuen
Wu Kangnian	吳康年	Ng Hong Lin
Wu Wenbiao	吳文表	Ng Man Piu
Wu Yanxia	吳雁霞	Ng Ngan Ha
Wu Yinghua	吳英華	Ng Ying Wa
Wu Quanyu	吳全祐	Ng Chyun Yau
Ye Ruli	葉汝立	Yip Y.L.
Ye Shuliang	葉樹良	Yip Sue Leong
Ye Wen	葉問	Yip Man
Yuan Lang	元朗	Yuen Long
Zheng Tianxiong	鄭天熊	Cheng Tin Hung
Zheng Yongguang	鄭榮光	Cheng Wing Kwong
Zhong Yueping	鍾岳平	Chung Ngok Ping

Notes

[1] Zhong Yueping also taught Zheng Tianxiong, the nephew of Zheng Yongguang (a disciple of Wu Jianquan). Zheng Tianxiong had a very successful school in Mongkok. He won open championships and taught generations of students who also performed well in tournaments against a variety of martial art stylists. He was responsible for training and assessing taiji coaches in the Hong Kong Public Parks. He founded the largest taiji organization in Hong Kong at that time: the Hong Kong Taiji Main Association.

[2] Years later, a group of disciples combined resources to purchase the flat on the top floor of Po Man Building, near King George V Garden, Jordan Road, for the Jianquan Association. This became the main school while the Wanchai school became a branch. Wu Dakui ran the Mongkok school.

[3] Note by Leroy Clark: After enduring decades of torture and imprisonment, Gongzao had nearly forgotten how to do the form. His leg injury would not allow him to do the form properly. His students report that Communist government officials had known that he was an adept in martial arts and, therefore, he had been deliberately tortured on his legs. Gongzao while imprisoned was only able to practice a qigong that did not require body movement. The guards were unable to keep him from doing at least that. During this politically charged period, torture methods for martial masters were selected to damage the masters' specialties, i.e., those who excelled in the use of the upper body limbs would be tortured on the upper limbs; those who excelled in leg work received trauma to the legs.

[4] January 1954 saw the much-publicized challenge of taijiquan's Wu Gongyi by White Crane stylist Chan Hak Fu. In Asia this was the fight of the century. It brought to the ring for the world to see for the first time the mysterious internal art against the widely accepted and understood external fighting art. The young, externalist Chan Hak Fu challenged taijiquan's senior, internalist Wu Gongyi, son of the widely known and respected Wu Jianquan. For an in-depth view of the challenge and impact, Yip and Clark (2002) Yip Y. and Clark, L. (2002). "Pivot." *Qi, the Journal of Traditional Eastern Health and Fitness*, (12) 3.

References

Wu, G.Z. (1933). *Taijiquan*. Hong Kong: Published by the Wu Family.

Wu, G.Z. (1984). *Wu family taijiquan*. Hong Kong: Published by the Wu Family.

Wu Family. (1995). *Wu style taijiquan and sabre*. Hong Kong: Published by the Wu Family.

chapter 3

A Comprehensive Introduction to
Sun Family Taiji Boxing Theory and Applications

by Jake Burroughs, B.A.

All photographs by Dana Benjamin. www.dkbimages.com

Introduction

Sun family taiji boxing is the most recently developed system of traditional taiji practiced today. Created by the legendary boxer Sun Lutang (1861-1933) during the golden years of Chinese pugilism, this martial art represents the culmination of over fifty years of martial experience compressed into one art form. According to his daughter, Sun Jianyun (1913-2003), of all his accomplishments Master Sun considered his taiji to be his "crowning achievement" within his lifetime—considering all of his accolades this is quite a statement to make. The following pages present the influential historical setting in which Sun Lutang developed his unique style and detail the fundamental principles upon which it was based.

Historical Setting

Sun Lutang was born in 1861 near Baoding in Hebei Province. His birth name was Sun Fuquan, and later in his life he took the name Han Zhai. Lutang was a name given to him by his bagua teacher Cheng Tinghua (1848-1900) in Sun's early 20's. Sun Lutang was a sick, weak child. Being born into a family of poverty it was common to see Sun on the streets begging for money. Eventually Sun discovered the arts of bajiquan and Shaolinquan, quickly progressing in these arts due to rigid practice sessions and hard work. As time progressed Sun dedicated himself to the arts of xingyiquan and baguazhang with the most combat-oriented teachers available. Guo Yunshen (1822-1898) and Li Kuiyuan taught him xingyi, while Cheng Tinghua tutored Sun in bagua. It did not take Sun long to master these arts, and eventually his reputation as a fighter spread throughout Asia. Even though Sun Lutang was small in size, he accepted any and all challenges, earning victories over *shuai chiao* (Chinese wrestling) players, as well as judo players from Japan.

Sun Lutang (1861-1933).

It is beyond the scope of this chapter to delve into all the details of Sun's extensive martial history. Suffice it to say that throughout the years Sun Lutang trained hundreds of fighters in xingyi and bagua, and also worked as a bodyguard where he acquired invaluable real world, hand-to-hand combat experience. Via these encounters, Sun refined his boxing and grappling skills, being meticulous in his note-taking and study of combat theory and application. He honed his own techniques accordingly with scrupulous detail to ensure he did not alter the principles of the traditional arts, yet made sure that the techniques he taught (as well as practiced) were efficient, accurate, and applicable. For a more detailed account of Sun Lutang's life history please refer to Tim Cartmell's translation of Sun's *A Study of Taijiquan* (2003, North Atlantic Books).

While visiting Beijing in the summer of 1914, the famous taiji teacher Hao Weizhen (1842-1920) fell ill. Sun invited Hao to stay with him so that he could help the teacher recover his health. Many people believe that Sun actually healed Hao, but Sun actually just took care of him—bringing the doctor to the house to treat him, running to fill herbal prescriptions, helping to feed Hao, etc.

When Hao recuperated, he taught Sun the Wu Yuxiang (1812-1880) taijiquan system as a token of gratitude. Already an accomplished master in his own right, Sun must have seen great benefit in learning this system—he immersed himself in practice day and night. After several years of intensive study, Sun decided to create his own system of taiji. He removed techniques he felt were useless and repetitive, and included many characteristics of bagua and xingyi that he had mastered over decades of practice. Sun Jianyun explained, "Sun Taiji has baguazhang's stepping method, xingyiquan's leg and waist methods, and taijiquan's body softness" (Cartmel, personal communication).

> "Sun's taijiquan emphasizes the importance of skill, sensitivity, and technique over the development of exceptional strength or speed."
> – Tim Cartmell, personal communication

Foundational Training

Sun Taiji follows the same sequence of movements in its form as the other taiji systems, and shares the major principles, such as Taiji's Thirteen Postures. Yet Sun Taiji is distinctive in that the practice of the form duplicates exactly how the techniques are applied in combat. Other styles of taiji tend to divide their study into form practice, then separate drills to develop applied martial theory and applications, whereas Sun Taiji combines all these aspects into one comprehensive martial system. Hence there is only one traditional form that is under eight minutes long when practiced in full. Though push hands (*tui shou*) is practiced within the Sun Taiji system, more emphasis is put on the actual application of force and technique with uncooperative partners, such as sparring and/or grappling drills. One must remember that push hands was originally much more combative in nature than what is commonly seen in today's martial society. Various levels would be taught from basic attempts to disrupt an opponent's balance, to all out wrestling incorporating joint immobilizations and strikes. Today some of these aspects are absent from taiji groups in an attempt to make push hands 'safer.' Unfortunately many of these teachers are missing the core ideas being taught in push hands type training.

All too often students become overwhelmed and confused with extensive curriculums. This is where Sun's genius comes into play: he developed the form to replicate fighting as much as one can for solo form practice. One example can be found within the footwork.

Sun Taiji employs the follow-up step from xingyi (the same footwork can be found in fencing, western boxing, and folk wrestling), which immediately trains whole body power. The upright stance (fighting posture), coupled with the rhythm of one foot advancing followed by the rear foot, and back again is unique to the Sun Taiji system, as other systems of thought emphasize low postures to build strength and flexibility. The use of whole body power is integral to any combat-oriented system, for if a practitioner weighs 180 pounds it is far more advantageous to use the full 180 pounds of mass, coupled with the velocity of the technique, than just to use the strength of an isolated appendage. This unification of body and technique is the epitome of force equals mass, times acceleration ($F=MA$), and is a vital trademark of Sun Taiji.

As stated earlier, Sun incorporated the circular footwork of bagua into his system of taiji. This afforded the practitioner circular mobility in technique, coupled with the linear footwork borrowed from xingyi. Bagua's stepping theory stresses constant changing, always trying to get to the opponent's back or side (the safest place to be in a fight where one's opponent cannot strike them), staying tight to the body and disrupting the opponent's center of balance. Once the opponent's center has been compromised, a throw, strike, joint manipulation, or kick can be applied. The bagua influence is most evident in the taiji technique of Repulse Monkey, which is akin to the single palm change.

Though these aspects of xingyi and bagua were incorporated into Sun Taiji, Sun Lutang maintained the taiji framework and principles as taught to him by Hao Weizhen. Redirection of force, sticking, and manipulating weak angles are all characteristics of taijiquan. Beyond the solo form and sparring/grappling practice, the curriculum also covered the Taiji's Thirteen Postures. These are not solo movements per se, but rather principles found throughout the form used to apply force in combat regardless of whether one is striking, or grappling (kicks and knees are included in striking, as joint manipulation is included into grappling in this instance). Broken down into the eight energies of force, the first four being the most prevalent, and then the five stepping methods, I offer a brief explanation for each as follows:

FOUR DIRECTIONS (si zheng)

1. **Ward Off (peng):** this represents any kind of rising energy generated by the body. Supported from below or to lift upward much like the hull of a boat supports the weight of the cargo when in water.
2. **Rollback (lu):** redirecting energy in a wedge-like manner, bringing force around the body, and maintaining central equilibrium (zhong ding) by turning around the center of the body.
3. **Press (ji):** applied straight into the opponent's body with a squeezing type

force that is sudden, not maintained. One analogy Tim Cartmell uses is like throwing a pebble onto the head of a drum.
4. **Push or Press Downward (*an*):** force applied in a downward trajectory generated by the whole body, not just the arms.

FOUR CORNERS (*si au*)

1. **Pluck (*cai*):** Much like when one tries to pick an apple from the tree: if one simply pulls on it, the stem does not break free. But once the slack is taken out of the pliable branch, all one needs to do is give it a quick jerk and the stem snaps off.
2. **Split (*lie*):** Where the upper body goes one direction and the lower body is led in the opposite direction. One visualization is the mechanics of a dead bolt lock where the one set of gears moves in one direction, while the other set is moved in the opposite direction.
3. **Elbow (*zhou*):** This concept is conveyed by using the elbow in any way possible from a strike, to coupling it with a throw or takedown. No one specific technique is localized; this is a general theory of applying the elbow.
4. **Lean (*kao*):** can be applied with any part of the body other than the arms or legs. Essentially to lean on, or into an opponent with one's own body. Think of it as a body stroke.

FIVE STEPPING METHODS (*wu ba fa*)

1. **Forward Advance (*qian jin*):** simply means to step forward.
2. **Backward Retreat (*hou tui*):** means just what the name implies, to step backwards.
3. **Look Left (*zuo gu*):** simply means to move to the left.
4. **Gaze Right (*you pan*):** to shift to the right.
5. **Central Equilibrium (*zhong ding*):** where one has one's weight/balance (equilibrium) centered evenly, where one is most stable.

Another unique facet of Sun Taiji is the *kai-he* movement found at the closing of each section within the form. Throughout the form there is a series of movements where the practitioner aligns the body, and "opens and closes" (*kai-he*) the shoulder girdle. One example of Sun's genius was that he knew people practicing a long form could not maintain proper structural integrity throughout, so he added these checkpoints to assist in proper structure to act as a reminder. Structure is key to martial usage, not to mention general overall health maintenance throughout daily life. In the martial sense if one does not have structure, then one cannot absorb, nor issue force efficiently. Keep in mind it is no different than building a house; no matter how well-built the frame is, without a solid foundation the frame will crumble to the earth.

Stillness in Motion

One of the first things a practitioner learns in the study of Sun Taiji is the *wuji* (carefree) posture. When practicing the form the student starts in wuji, and ends in wuji. Wuji is not a static pose, but rather a set of alignments used to ensure proper physical structure is attained and maintained. Some points of reference in regards to wuji:

CAREFREE POSTURE (*wuji zhuang*)

- Head is suspended from the crown as if being extended by a balloon attached to a string connected to the crown. This draws in the chin, preventing the chin from protruding, as well as properly extending the cervical vertebrae. Some of the classics refer to this alignment as "tucking the ears."
- Shoulders are rounded and relaxed, ensuring the chest does not stick out, nor does it slouch. The shoulder blades should feel as if they are going to slough off the back.
- Sternum is kept up as if a hook is underneath it gently pulling up.
- Pelvic girdle has a quality of floating in a fish bowl. This means that the pelvis should not be tucked, nor should the butt be sticking out. There should be no left or right flexion, either. Relaxed and ready to move in any direction.
- Knees are slightly bent and tracking the toes, which means wherever the toes point, the knees should be pointing in the exact same direction. Otherwise a sheering force is put on the knee and can do quite a bit of damage to the soft tissue supporting the knee.
- Feet are flat on the ground, weight evenly distributed with a slight shift towards the balls of the feet.
- Arms are relaxed at the sides with the hands open and slightly curved as if palming a basketball.

The open/closing action done at the close of each section within the form is essentially a wuji checkpoint that allows the practitioner to check the posture without interrupting the flow of practice. The only physical difference is with open/closing the arms are maintained in front of the body as if holding a ball at chest height, instead of the arms at the sides as in the posture of wuji.

According to Sun Jianyun, her father had the students stand in the Three Powers Posture (*santi shi*) more so than wuji. Santi is from the xingyi boxing school and is basically a more combative version of wuji. In the santi posture, the student stands in more of a combat posture with a lead arm and leg, maintaining the same pointers found above with wuji, but with more of a martial intent and focus. The goal with santi training is to relax in a combative posture, engaging only the skeletal muscles to stand in the proper posture. The characteristics practiced in santi are found throughout the Sun Taiji form: again posture and structure being key to the proper usage of combat-oriented martial arts—not to mention all the positive health benefits gained from proper posture throughout daily living!

Other than wuji and santi, there are not many basics in Sun Taiji. Again everything the student needs is found within the framework of the form and the practice of applications that are extrapolated from the movements of the form. Sun Lutang had a wonderful reputation throughout China so most of the very experienced, knowledgeable martial artists that trained under Sun were already quite well-versed in the basics of martial combat from their previous training.

Taiji as Combative Art

The structure and flow of the form also attests to Sun's intelligent design. The techniques that one would most often use in combat were repeated throughout the entire form, for example Too Lazy to Tie Coat, Hands Strum the Pipa, Single Whip, Repulse Monkey, and Brush Knee Twist Step. Brush Knee Twist Step, and Single Whip alone were the initial movements in every section of the form! The easier techniques were also usually practiced towards the beginning of the form, with the more challenging maneuvers reserved for the final couple of sections.

This is a prime example why many traditionalists take exception to modern wushu variations on forms, because techniques are in a certain order, placed carefully within the form that act as keys integral to unlocking the usage of the movement. For instance certain footwork patterns in the solo form are indicators as to how one should apply a kick in combat. If the player does not step to this specific angle, the kick is rendered useless.

All systems of taiji are combative in nature, training to issue maximum force while using minimal effort, and as much as 80% of the techniques practiced are grappling (or counter-grappling) in nature. Sun Lutang fought many high-level grappling experts in his time (Sun's birthplace, Baoding, was famous for its wrestlers), so by the time he developed Sun Taiji he was well versed in grappling and counter-grappling techniques and the theory on which they are based. As it is today, it was 120 years ago when two combatants engaging in hand-to-hand combat used strikes to close the distance and come into contact with their opponent. Once contact was made (usually in what is now called the "clinch range") the most proficient fighters used their grappling skills to throw, sweep, or takedown their opponent. This strategy afforded several benefits for the fighter; as any kind of throw is extremely destructive in nature. By utilizing proper technique and leverage, a smaller, weaker fighter can have an advantage over a larger, stronger opponent. This may not be the case if he chooses to stand and trade blows with his opponent, since the larger, stronger fighter will more likely prevail. That is simple physics. Also keep in mind that at the time, the majority of average civilians in China were laborers who relied on their hands to earn money. A broken hand or foot caused by a fight (or practice for that matter) rendered a person not only injured, but also took him out of work for a period of time.

Throws and the variations such as sweeps, takedowns, and joint manipulation techniques were preferred because they could be practiced without having to "pull" one's technique (as in the case with strikes), and in actual combat a throw on the hard ground can decisively end a confrontation. It should come as no surprise to the taiji student, or any martial artist for that matter, that the majority of techniques in Sun Taiji are grappling-based. This is human nature.

One needs to look no further than to watch two untrained people fight. Inevitably one will initiate contact with strikes, while the other will try to protect himself by bringing his arms up to cover his head and face, while simultaneously trying to grab and hold his opponent in an effort to control the strikes that are overwhelming him. Once this is accomplished, the opponents are considered to be in the "clinch" range. Strikes are limited within the clinch so grappling takes precedence as one closes with the opponent, enabling one to join mutual centers of gravity. Once one has joined these centers of gravity, it becomes much easier to manipulate the opponent's "dead angle" (the angle representing the weakest directions in which a person can be put off-balance). In combat we are constantly trying to control our opponent's dead angle, while concurrently attempting to hide our own.

Sun Lutang realized that the nature of true combat fell within these parameters and was mindful of including close quarter combat theory and application into his system of taiji. This was already second nature to him as his xingyi training included many *kao die* (literally "knock downs") type takedowns which are quick and percussive. Also, he learned bagua from Cheng Tinghua, whose foundation was in *shuai chiao* (Chinese wrestling/grappling), and who was considered one of the best wrestlers of his era. This is not to say striking and kicking are not practiced in the art, as they certainly are very well represented; however, I simply wish to shed some light on the role of grappling in traditional Chinese martial arts.

TECHNICAL SECTION

Rollback / Elbow Strike

1a) White sets up his attack with a quick back-fist type strike (it is the intention to get the opponent to react, hence the big movement of the back-fist), which of course black blocks.

1b-c) White uses his left hand to parry black's block, while simultaneously stepping through with his left foot. White has his hand "hooked" onto black's elbow crease so that when black pushes back against white's pressure, it assists white in executing the upward elbow (*zhou*). Usually this elbow lands because of the speed and aggressiveness of the technique, but for argument's sake black deflects the incoming elbow.

1d) Again using the pressure from black's defense, white applies rollback by bringing black's arm across his body. It may be necessary to shift, or lean slightly back while parrying the opponent's arm. That is fine as long as one's structure is not compromised.

1e) White finishes with a simple projection, but really any number of techniques can be applied here.

Reverse Angle of Elbow Strike - Rollback

2a-d) Close up and reverse angle to previous technique.

Joint Manipulation

3a) Here is a joint manipulation application utilizing the splitting principle (*lie*). Tim (black) and Jake (white) are jockeying for position in grappling range. Neither has a better position, yet notice how black's right arm is on the inside gate of white's left arm.

3b) Black obtains wrist control with his left hand, and sets up the arm drag with his right hand. Notice black reaching high (superior) on white's tricep for the arm drag.

3c) Black switches his grip by sliding along white's arm. As black brings white's arm across his body (to black's right), black's right hand slips down to obtain wrist control, while his left hand slides up just superior to the elbow joint. This is obviously done quickly and decisively, but arm drags are deceiving to their victims in that by the time one notices their position has been compromised—it is too late.

3d) Black maneuvers under white's arm, extending it, applying pressure at the fulcrum which is white's elbow, using white's arm as a lever. Notice how black has also twisted white's arm to black's right. This rotation tightens the joint lock by taking all the slack out of the arm.

Single Whip

4a-b) White attacks black from behind and puts him in an over-arm bear hug. Black lowers his center of gravity.

4c) Black lifts up on the elbows by using his legs, not the strength of his arms.

4d-e) Black steps behind white with his left leg. It is key to keep close contact with the opponent here. This is where black joins centers. Without doing so, black would not be able to disrupt a bigger, stronger opponent's structure. To finish the takedown, black simply turns to his left and white falls from the pressure of black's turn, coupled with the fact that white's mobility is compromised because black has stepped behind him.

Fist Under Elbow

5a) Black offers a right lead jab, which white slips (*zuo gu*, or "look left").

5b) White strikes low with a straight punch to black's ribs ("fist under elbow").

5c) Black drops his right elbow to block, or possibly as a reaction to white's strike.

5d) White steps behind black, taking his left hand and draping it (thumb down) onto black's eyebrow ridge. Again notice the proximity of the bodies, joining centers once again.

5e) White simply turns his body to the left using a classic "eyebrow mop" type technique as a follow-up. White has superior leverage the closer to the top of black's head he gets, again blocking black from stepping out by using white's left leg. It is very important to use a spiral type action with the "eyebrow mop" takedown, not just turning in a circle.

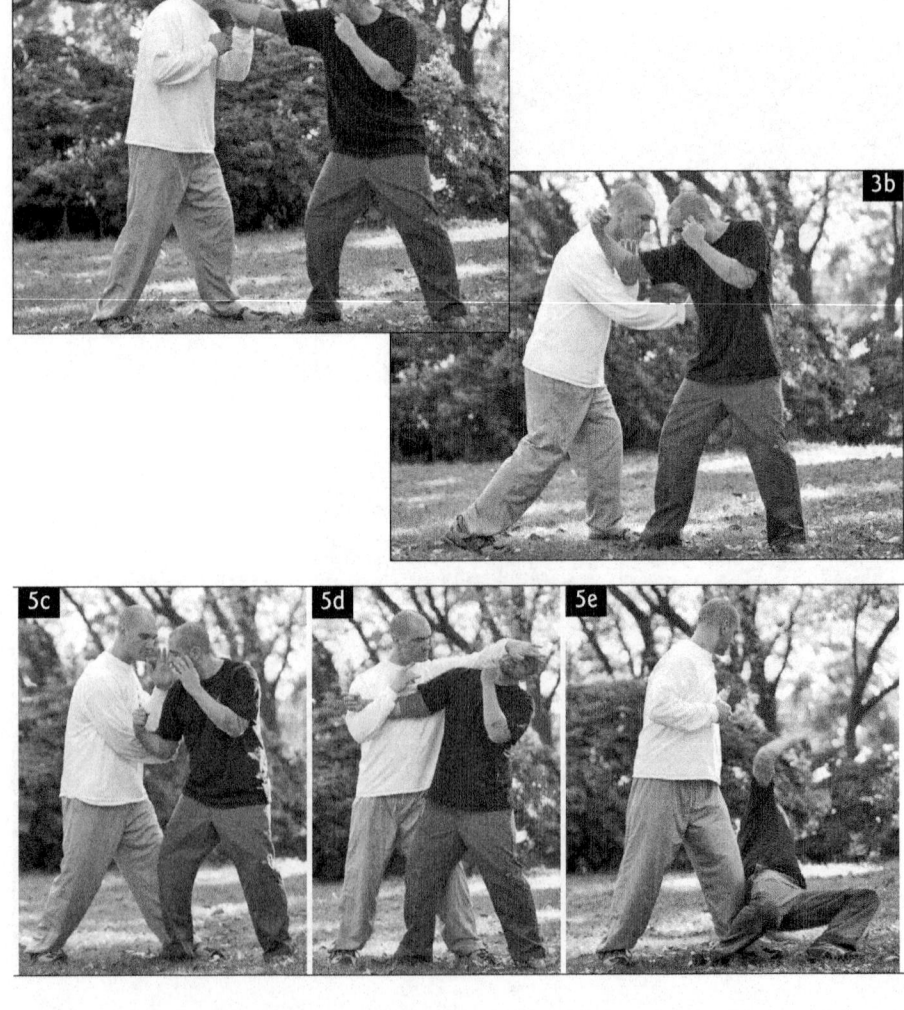

Open and Closed Fighting Postures

6a) The ending postures for each section of the routine, as divided by Tim Cartmell; open-close (*kai-he*) is used to realign and reposition the student ensuring the chest is up, head suspended, shoulder blades relaxed, elbows in and down, hands up, all the attributes of wuji stance but with the hands held in a fighting position.

6b) Kai-he is the standard fighting position: hands up protecting the head, elbows down and in protecting the body, eyes forward, weight distributed 50/50 on the legs, weight towards the balls of the feet, knees bent and relaxed, and intent forward.

Part Wild Horse's Mane

7a) Here black initiates a lead arm hook, which white steps off-line to avoid (*you pan*, or "gaze right") while simultaneously striking with a cross-palm strike.

7b) White quickly steps in and behind black with his left leg, while keeping his left arm taut, thus disrupting black's structure. Notice there is no gap between the two bodies.

7c) Exploiting black's dead angle, white simply shifts his weight forward to complete the takedown. It is not necessary for white to turn the body or push with the arm. Positioning the body correctly (with no gaps) joins centers with the opponent. White's leg prevents black from stepping out, and the pressure into black's dead angle is what creates the takedown.

Repulse Monkey

8a-b) Black and white square-off in a right lead closed stance. White initiates with a lead arm hook which black covers, and counters with a lead arm palm strike in an effort to get white to react with a block.

8c) Black quickly swings his right arm over, down, and through to obtain his right underhook. Simultaneously black's left arm clamps down over top of white's arm, and black has left arm control at the elbow, squeezing white's arm in-between his body and his left arm. Notice here how black has also toed in his right foot setting up the throw.

8d) Black turns to his left, pulling on white's right elbow, lifting up with his underhook, and slipping his hip in under white's center of gravity for the hip throw.

8e) Black finishes with a devastating throw, which flows nicely into a superior position with white's arm extended, and a knee on white's ribs. Black can strike, work to submit with an arm bar, or continue the fight on the ground. Repulse Monkey is repeated twice in the Sun Taiji set emphasizing the importance, and applicability of this technique. The influence of Sun's bagua is found here as Repulse Monkey is essentially the same movement/ technique as the single palm change in Sun bagua.

Lotus Kick

9a-b) Black and white square off in an open posture, where white throws a lead arm committed jab, which black quickly slips and parries.

9c) Black throws a left hand towards white's face to get him to react with his left hand. Since black is grabbing white's right hand it is natural instinct for white to pull back on his arm when it is grabbed.

9d) Black shoots his right hand across white's body and uses his right hip as a leverage point. By pivoting and twisting in this manner, white's structure is compromised.

9e-f) Black finishes by stepping his right leg behind white and using a combination

Step to the Seven Stars

10a) Step to the Seven Stars is an entry technique to get inside your opponent's guard. Here white simply does a basic palm strike to black's head causing him to react with a basic block.

10b) White steps forward and weaves his left hand under black's block, opening his guard.

10c) This creates an opening where white can again execute any application, but here employs an elbow technique (remember taiji is a close-quarter fighting system, so elbows, knees, and grappling are heavily emphasized).

Turn the Body - Ambush the Tiger

11a) Black attacks with a lead arm palm strike, which white quickly blocks.

11b) Black checks white's block, and throw's another palm strike towards white's face causing him to block with his left arm now.

11c) Black pulls white's left arm across his body, maintaining wrist control on white's right wrist. Notice how black has toed in his right foot in preparation for the throw, and has white's weight towards his heels to circumvent any counter measures.

11d) Crossing white's arm, keeping them extended, and loading him onto his back like a sack of potatoes, black now shoots in his hip getting under white's center of gravity and joins centers.

11e) To finish the throw, black loads the weight of white onto him, straightens his leg and turns his right shoulder in the direction toward his left foot.

Be careful with this throw as your partner has no way of slapping out from this very large, hard throw!

Not Just for Fighters

The recent popularity of practicing taiji as a meditative, yoga-like exercise was non-existent in Sun Lutang's lifetime. That is not to say Sun Taiji cannot be practiced by those looking to reap the rewards of non-combative aspects of the art. The upright posture and high stance are ideal for those with back, knee, or hip problems. The complete form takes less than ten minutes to perform so it does not necessarily require a lot of energy, yet the faster pace in which Sun Taiji is practiced offers a light cardiovascular workout as well. The movements are simple and easy to remember, and are low impact for those with health issues or the elderly. The emphasis on correct posture, and the repeated twisting and bending of the waist is wonderful exercise for the body's core. Remember, any physical exercise will harvest positive results, and any exercise is better than none. Sun Taiji can be practiced with as little, or as much, intensity as the practitioner desires.

Sun Taiji is a complete martial system and can be adapted to almost anyone. It is a beautiful form, as well as an effective martial art. Maintaining many familiar aspects of the internal arts (*nei jia*) while simultaneously creating a new approach to the study of taiji, Sun Lutang was truly ahead of his time with the creation of Sun Taijiquan. Though rare in the West, Sun Taiji is gaining in popularity as more teachers are offering lessons, seminars, and classes throughout the United States, and Europe. It is my hope that Sun Taiji is made available to more people throughout the world, as it is a wonderful martial art with bountiful health benefits.

Glossary

Baoding	保定	Santi Shi	三體式
Cheng Tinghua	程廷華	Sun Family Taijiquan	孫家太極拳
Guo Yunshen	郭雲深	Sun Fuquan	孫福全
Hao Weizhen	郝為真	Sun Jianyun	孫劍雲
he	合	Sun Lutang	孫祿堂
kai	開	Wu Yuxiang	武禹襄
Li Kuiyuan	李魁元	Wuji	無極

Acknowledgments

The author would like to thank Tim Cartmell for his diligent teachings, never ending patience, and forthright approach to the study and teaching of the Chinese martial arts. Also thanks to Tim and Anthony Natale for assistance in the application photographs. Plus, deep gratitude to Dana Benjamin for her amazing work with photographs in all the authors works, and her support and input behind the scenes.

chapter 4

Xiong Style Taiji in Taiwan:
Historical Development & A Photographic Exposé Featuring Master Lin Jianhong

by Michael A. DeMarco, M.A.

Photographs of Xiong Yanghe alongside the cover of a special commemorative edition published for his 100th birthday anniversary ("Commemorative," 1987). Photographs from the author's collection.
Photographs courtesy of Robert Lin-I Yu, except where noted.

Introduction

In the thickly branched tree representing taijiquan's growth over the centuries, some branches are stronger than others, and some hold higher positions than others. This chapter introduces a relatively rare branch in the Yang Family tradition that is associated with Xiong Yanghe (1888-1981). Before delving into aspects of what is now called the Xiong Style, we must first ask ourselves what we can learn from studying the lives of main lineage representatives. How can their theories and practices of taiji influence our overall understanding of the art? Hopefully such research can offer a better historical perspective while enriching both our understanding and practice of the art.

The following text presents aspects of lineage that play a role in formulating a definition of taijiquan. Following a general overview of the early Yang Family lineage, we will look closely at the two main branches that stem directly from the Yang Style founder, Yang Luchan (1799~1872), his sons and grandsons, who were so influential in the initial growth of taiji in China. Since the focus of this chapter is on Xiong Style, it is necessary to look at Xiong's teachers and these main predecessors who formed the main trunk of the taiji evolutionary tree.

China's socio-political setting during the lives of Yang Luchan and Xiong Yanghe was rife with foreign invasions and civil strife. This difficult period—marred by the decaying decades of the last dynasty (Qing, 1644-1911) and the following decades up to the founding of the People's Republic of China in 1949—presents an overwhelming wealth of information that played into the thoughts and actions of each taiji master mentioned above. Each master has his own story to tell. This chapter is a brief synopsis of Xiong Yanghe's story, supplemented with information and photographic illustrations provided by Mr. Lin Jianhong, a leading Xiong Style instructor teaching today in Taipei, Taiwan.

The Question of Taiji Lineage

Many newcomers are thrilled to begin learning taiji. If they have a decent teacher and a growing interest in the art, they eventually delve deeper into its history, theory, and practice. However, they soon find themselves entangled in a mesh of lineage lines. Who taught whom? What are the differences between the original Chen Family Style and evolving branches? What did the main instructors actually teach versus the curricula taught by their students in following generations? In the end, what do we really learn from the academic grasp of lineages, names, dates, and a stock of stories which may be true or false?

When we approach taijiquan's history, we are usually given our initial glimpse through our first teacher. This provides an introduction to taiji. Depending on the teacher, the art may be totally focused on its health nurturing aspects suitable for aged retirees in their quest to keep fit. Some teachers focus on it as a fighting art, suitable for bodyguards, military, and police. Others can teach both aspects of the art in varied proportions.

There are other layers to consider in our desire to understand taiji. All teachers have unique qualities in their form and function: movements, stances, fighting techniques, and applied skills. It is easy to see great differences among beginning students in their awkward execution of taiji forms, but even teachers of the same lineage and generation exhibit their own individual flavors, although it may be in the most subtle ways. Of course it is important to discern the dissimilarity in movements as either a variant application performed according to taiji principles, or an incorrect movement based on faulty understanding of application and performed contrary to the taiji principles.

Often the more we learn about taiji the more confusing it gets! There is an old tale that originated in India that may offer some help in our view of taiji lineages and practice. It is the story of six blind men who were asked to describe the nature of an elephant, with each person feeling the elephant's various body parts, such as its tusk, tail, trunk, leg, ear, or side. Of course, all their conclusions vary because of their different perspectives. The "elephant" they envisioned appeared like a spear, wall, snake, tree, fan or rope. They may endlessly argue over their viewpoints, or use them to better understand what an elephant really is in its completeness.

If we really seek to know taiji thoroughly, we need to go beyond relative half-truths to get a broader perspective. A study of the leading standard-bearers of each main lineage is certainly helpful for the broad view. On a more detailed level, we can look closely at the main teachers within one specific lineage. The learning process takes many years, and we eventually see how our concept of taiji continually evolves.

Blind Monks Examining an Elephant
by Itcho Hanabusa
Japanese Ukiyo-e print illustration from Buddhist parable
showing blind monks examining an elephant. Dated 1888.
Library of Congress. Call # Illus. in H67 [Asian RR]

Early Yang Style Lineage Representatives

Yang Luchan was born in 1799 in Yongnian County, Hebei Province. Although he was a man of humble origins and illiterate, he loved martial arts. He probably studied Shaolin boxing when very young but later was drawn to the Chen Village in Henan Province with the desire to study Chen Family Taijiquan. Although there are a number of stories regarding Luchan's study in Chen Village, the most probable themes are: 1) he worked as a servant and studied Chen Taiji under Chen Changxing (1771-1853) for most likely ten years or so, becoming extraordinarily proficient in the art, 2) he returned to his home village and taught the art to many there, and 3) moved to Beijing where he gained a reputation as "Invincible Yang" and taught the Manchu royal family and bodyguards. Of course, his unique flavor of taiji became known as the Yang Style.

Whether factual or fictional, stories regarding Yang Luchan leave no doubt that he possessed fighting skills of the highest order. What he taught and to whom is another matter. It certainly would be logical for him to follow ancient precedent and teach the higher aspects of the art only to those closest to him.

When Yang Luchan died in 1872, two of his sons carried on the family's taiji tradition. Both were naturally gifted, mentally and physically, to receive full transmission of their father's knowledge, and both practiced with dedication under a demanding training regimen. The brothers came to exhibit very different personalities. Yang Banhou (1837-1890), the elder son, had a character often described as hard and fierce, which manifested in his love of sparring. The younger son, Yang Jianhou (1839-1917), was friendly and gentle, a personality which attracted a large number of students.

Although Yang Shaohou (1862-1930) was the first son of Yang Jianhou, Shaohou studied primarily with his uncle, Yang Banhou. Shaohou followed his uncle in temperament and fighting style. Both were harsh teachers and only a relatively small number of students became dedicated disciples. It seems they used the combative elements of Yang Luchan's methods as the main guideline for their own practice, which included high speed execution of techniques, jumps, and varied kicks, as well as the psychological use of expressions and vocal sound. As Douglas Wile writes: "Writings tracing their origins to Yang [Banhou] are our closest link to Yang [Luchan] and to the richness of the art before it moved into the mainstream of Chinese culture in the twentieth century" (Wile, 1996: 93).

Yang Jianhou's second son was Yang Chengfu (1883-1936). He and his brother Shaohou taught taijiquan at the Beijing Physical Culture Research Institute from 1914 until 1928. They were pioneers in bringing instruction to the general public. Chengfu moved to Shanghai in 1928 and taught many. Over the years, Chengfu's particular style became the most widespread. He eliminated some of the more vigorous techniques from the long routine and taught others to practice at a slow, even tempo. Although he certainly retained the teachings of his father, uncle, and grandfather, Chengfu's public style became popular for its health nurturing benefits.

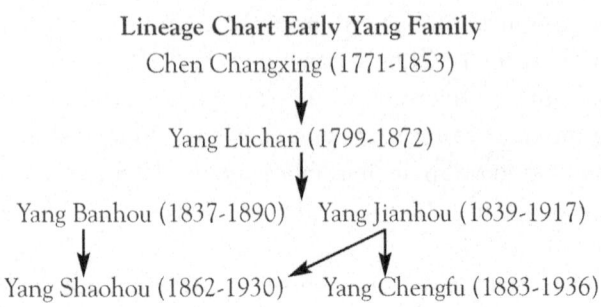

Lineage Chart Early Yang Family

The five Yang family members discussed in the preceding paragraphs lived during a time of drastic change in China. Their lives cover 137 years, from the birth of Yang Luchan in 1799 to the death of Yang Chengfu in 1936. A brief overview of Chinese history during this period will be helpful for understanding the development of taijiquan, as well as other Chinese martial arts that have become popular in the modern era. The realities of those decades influenced the ways the early taiji masters viewed their art, how they taught, and to whom they would transmit their knowledge and skills.

The Effect of Time and Place for Early Yang Style Taiji

What inspired Yang Luchan to study martial arts? Was Chen Family boxing very different from other family styles developed in other villages? Actually, to have a group of villagers with a common surname practicing boxing within their courtyards was not a rare phenomenon in the latter half of the Qing Dynasty (1644-1911). Philip Kuhn (1970) details the growth of local militia, rebels, bandit groups, and secret societies in his excellent work, *Rebellion and Its Enemies in Late Imperial China: Militarization and Social Structure, 1796-1864*. Chen Village is only one example of a village that built up their walls and fighting tradition for protection from attack and theft from outsiders, such as local bandits.

There are "... two basic types of militia institutions in Chinese society—those born of state prescription and those born of the needs of natural social units..." (Kuhn, 1970: 35). The rise of local defense groups became more and more important as the Qing government and its military and police structures fragmented under internal and external pressures. Their rise was in direct response to the unstable socio-political climate.

In the 18th century there was a growing domestic discontent throughout China as the population increased to a point where food production could not keep pace. "Population growth inevitably surpassed increased food production, and the standard of living began to decline. Spreading corruption and indolence in government made conditions worse" (Hucker, 1975: 302). Besides an anti-foreign sentiment for the Manchu rulers who conquered China and ruled from 1644 to 1911, the general population felt the government had lost the Mandate of Heaven and were unfit to rule. Popular uprisings became endemic, erupting into major social upheavals such as the rebellion by the White Lotus Society (1793-1804). Even more devastating was the Taiping Rebellion (1851-1864) in which nearly thirty million lost their lives bringing destruction to fifteen provinces (Wakeman, 1977: 156). By the mid-19th century, in some provinces "two-thirds of the population was reported dead or missing" (Wakeman, 1977: 155).

For centuries, China had thought itself to be the most civilized state in the world. However, rebellions, famine, and floods took a great toll on the government and society during the 19th century. China's image of itself gradually changed. It was no longer a country of strength and wealth, and foreign countries took advantage of this frailty. With the intrusion of European traders and missionaries, China soon felt its weakness in regard to modern ways of warfare and international business. Over the decades, the Portuguese, Dutch, British, French, Americans, Russians, and Japanese applied more pressure on China as they tried to profit through unequal trade agreements, acquisition of port cities, opium trafficking, and a siphoning off of the dwindling reserves of silver. Foreign powers took advantage of a China that had already been weakened from within.

In parallel with a long list of internal rebellions is a list of wars with foreign countries, such as the Opium War (1839-1842), the Anglo-Chinese War (1856-1860), and the Sino-French War (1884-1885). The foreign encroachments were destructive, but their real significance lies in the resulting treaties, which were unequal in that they gave great advantage to the foreign powers at a high cost to the Chinese. The Sino-Japanese War (1884-1895) provided a "profound psychological shock," since it "did more than any other crisis to force the Chinese to evaluate their own strengths and weaknesses" (Wakeman, 1977: 192). Above all, each treaty humiliated the Chinese, and many started to seek solutions to resolve the problems caused by the decades of internal strife and foreign influence.

During the later half of the 19th century, many political and intellectual leaders were engaged in discussing ways to restore the Qing Imperial system or a new political system through "self-strengthening." It seems most of the attempts either failed or made matters worse. For example, one idea was to use the resentment against imperialist expansion to encourage the Boxer Uprising (1900-1901) against foreign embassies. This was doomed to failure. "Thousands of young men began to practice the stylized exercises of Shaolin and [bagua] boxing—exercises that were supposed to release their [*qi*] (pneuma) and invest them with strength so awesome that it repelled foreign bullets" (Wakeman, 1977: 217). Even a Chinese military general "simply scoffed at their claims of invulnerability to firearms," and "put 50 Boxers of the Golden Belt Society to the test by lining them up against a wall and shooting them" (Wakeman, 1977: 218). The Boxers' leader was caught and decapitated. Their defeat brought new demands upon the Chinese and resulted in even greater loss of power.

As the Beijing government was losing control of the provinces, there was a corresponding growth of power in local areas, often associated with the provinces themselves. Frederic Wakeman notes that "the provincial governors of the early 1900s, took on more and more of the military and fiscal functions that had once belonged to the central government" (Wakeman, 1977: 232). In nearly half of China's provinces "military men became governors immediately after the [Wuhan Revolution (1911)], or within the following two or three months. Moreover, the troops in the various provinces... were largely recruited from within the provinces in which they served; their loyalties were strongly provincial and personal, so that provincial military leaders had, in effect, personal armies at their disposal...." (Sheridan, 1977: 147).

As private armies developed—some small and some large—warfare increased. "Between 1916 and 1928, the struggle among independent militarists—warlords—tore China into fragments, and the formal political machinery of the republic that had succeeded the monarchy—the parliament, ministries, and so forth—became largely irrelevant to the realities of Chinese political life. At the head of their personal armies, the warlords dominated districts, provinces, and regions, and warred with neighboring generals for additional territory and revenues" (Sheridan, 1977: 20).

War was endemic during this Warlord Period (1916-1928). One writer has "counted more than 400 large and small civil wars in the province of Szechwan alone" (Sheridan, 1977: 88). With such chaos in the land, how would it be possible to reintegrate China under a modern, unified national government? Each warlord faction operated according to his own interests and political ends. One interesting aspect of note is how soldiers were trained. Decorum varied greatly according to group. Some warlords demanded that troops be highly trained while acting with utmost compassion toward the general population. Their honorable code of discipline stressed good treatment toward all and maintaining personal restraint from vices associated with soldiers of poor character. General Feng Yuxiang (1882-1948), for example, "demanded extraordinary physical fitness, and subjected his officers and men to constant and rigorous training to achieve it. ... He prohibited drinking, gambling, visiting prostitutes, even swearing" (Sheridan, 1977: 74). At the other end of the spectrum were other warlords and their troops who drank alcohol, raped, and robbed at will.

Postage stamp issued by the Republic of China "To Commemorate Unification," bearing the portrait of Generalissimo Chiang Kai-shek. *Courtesy of iStockphoto.com.*

In the midst of the dynamic political and military flux of the warlord period, loyalties often shifted between warlords, as well as their officers and troops (Sheridan, 1977: 58). A few factions grew strong while many became weak and disintegrated or were absorbed. Eventually there were two main political parties contending for supremacy: the Nationalists (Guomintang) under the leadership of General Chiang Kai-shek (1887-1975), and the Chinese Communist Party, under Mao Zedong (1893-1976). Initially they worked together to end the warlord period and drive out the Japanese, but their differences in political ideology brought on an inevitable civil war (1927-1949).

Chiang Kai-shek, raised during the warlord period, had learned "to revolve all his politics about the concept of force... He had gown up in a time of treachery and violence.... There were few standards of human decency his warlord contemporaries did not violate. They obeyed no law but power..." (Schurmann and Schell, 1967: 236). Mao also faced this hard reality, and his often quoted statement is: "Political power grows out of the barrel of a gun." Chiang and Mao fought it out until the Communists emerged victorious in 1949.

A "protracted revolutionary transformation" lasted for more than a century, "but in many ways the critical period was the 37 years, 1912-1949, from the fall of the monarchy and founding of a republic to the establishment of the People's Republic of China by the Communists. During this republican period, disintegration and disorder were at their maximum" (Sheridan, 1977: 4). All of the early Yang Style Taijiquan masters lived during this revolutionary transformation, and there are some common factors in their lives that influenced their teaching.

The greatest single factor in taijiquan's development was its association with defense. There were centuries of banditry, small and large scale rebellions, and secret society activities throughout China. Particularly, rural areas lacked protection by the national army or police, so martial arts training was utilized for regional and local defense. The Chen Village is only one example of how a family style martial art developed within a walled village, although it is a famous example. It is the site of the original Chen Family Style Taijiquan, which was famed for its superior boxing system. Chen family representatives, such as Chen Changxing (1771-1853) and Chen Gengyun (1799-1872), were employed as elite bodyguards and for cargo transport security personnel; Chen Yenxi (1848-1929) trained the son of the first Republican president Yuan Shikai, and was also the family bodyguard for scholar-official Du Youmei in Boai, Henan. Du's son, Du Yuzi (1886-1990) became a disciple of Chen Yenxi.

Fear is a great motivator. People had to protect their food stocks as well as their lives. Many trained hard and often. They also feared a shift in loyalties, so they were cautious about whom they taught. Usually the ties were personal (teaching family or village members) and, under circumstances involving a larger area, ties would be provincial, where common dialect and social customs reinforced some bonding.

The decades of great social change brought changes in relationships. Chen Style moved outside its home village, and others, such as Yang Luchan, came to learn Chen Taiji. Luchan and his son Banhou taught Manchu imperial guards and garrison troops. Some teaching was done privately and some publically. "When asked why the [Guangping] students of the Yang family showed both hard and soft techniques in their style, whereas the [Beijing] students showed only soft techniques, [Banhou] replied that the [Beijing] students were mainly wealthy aristocrats, and that, after all, there was a difference between Chinese and Manchus, implying a policy of passive resistance to the alien dynasty by imparting only half of taijiquan transmission" (Wile, 1983: ix).

When Yang Chengfu was born (1883), his grandfather Luchan had already been dead eleven years, and his uncle Banhou died when Chengfu was nine. As a result, Chengfu's training was somewhat different than that of his brother Yang Shaohou. Shaohou and Banhou were noted for their rough boxing. Internationally, Shaohou's style is not as well known as Yang Chengfu's. The difficulties surrounding his life led him to commit suicide in 1930 (Yun, 2006: 55).

The lives of the Chen Style and early Yang Style Taiji masters reflect their times. The leading figures were highly involved with defense on a local, provincial, and sometimes national level. The need for true, highly effective martial skills was ingrained in the consciousness of all facing life and death struggles in their daily lives. Famed martial art teachers, like Yang Luchan, were placed in a quandary between the desire to keep their highest knowledge from "outsiders" and the wish to help close family members and friends. They also had to make a living during difficult times.

There was another motivation for teaching that is often overlooked. It involves the many decades of humiliating treatment at the hands of foreign countries which forced China to give concessions away while losing their own land, wealth, and dignity. The Chinese became known as the "sick man of Asia." That phrase features in the Bruce Lee film *Fist of Fury* (1971), and the Jet Li film *Fearless* (2006). The idea of teaching martial arts for health fit in well with the "self-strengthening" movement in the early 20th century. The country needed to become strong, as did its people.

Xiong Yanghe and His Unique Contributions to Taijiquan

Early on, Yang Luchan and his sons were exhibiting different modes of instruction. They had an array of students: family members, military officials, Manchu guards, other martial art instructors, the affluent and the peasant. Each held the Yang Family tradition and could tailor their instruction according to the student-teacher relationship.

Personalities also played a role in teaching methods as well as in the selection of students. There were polar yin-yang characteristics shown between Yang Banhou (*yang*) and Yang Jianhou (*yin*), and in the following generation between Yang Shaohou (*yang*) and Yang Chengfu (*yin*)! Shaohou's style was physically and mentally demanding, plus he would not pull punches with his students. Yang Chengfu's style became the most popular because of his more pleasing character and teaching methods. The slower tempo and modifications he made were suitable for a greater number of people, such as the elderly. His teaching had a great impact on national "self-strengthening" by bringing health to thousands.

What is Xiong Yanghe's place in this development? Within the Yang Taiji linage, he took his teachings to Taiwan following the exodus of the Chinese Nationalists to Taiwan in 1949 and became a major influence in the spread of taiji throughout the island. When he passed away in 1981, he and his senior disciples had taught over ten thousand students. His style continues to spread via his disciples, and his unique system is now referred to as Xiong Style Taiji. Xiong's story proves interesting for his unique place in taiji as well as his personal life.

Xiong was born on September 29, 1888 in Jiangsu Province, in Funing County. His father, Xiong Weizhen, passed the provincial examination (*juren* military degree) during the late Qing Dynasty. Yanghe studied martial arts first with his father, then his father hired instructors for his young son: at age 12, a Shaolin master named Liu He and his disciple Liu Zhongfang came to teach; at age 15, Master Yin Wanbang for Jiangnan Eight Harmonies Boxing system. These had a martial influence from Gan Fengchi. When Xiong was 20, "Miraculous Hand" Tang Dianqing (1850-1926) was hired to teach. These teachers provided young Xiong with an excellent foundation in Shaolin boxing and may have given Xiong his first exposure to taijiquan.

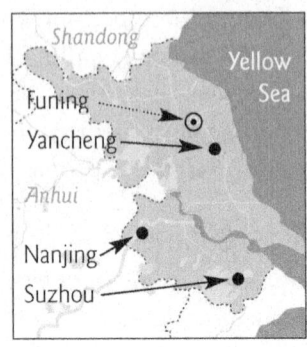

Jiangsu Province is on China's east coast.
Xiong Yanghe was born in Funing,
which is in Yancheng municipality.

Xiong had hands-on fighting experience as he helped his father maintain township security. He found himself all too often fighting with gangsters. When he was 19 years old, he was the local boxing champion in the "no holds barred" competitions held on raised platforms (*leitai*), as seen in the movie *Fearless*. Because of his powerful kicks, Xiong earned the nickname of "Funing Legs." Such experiences gave him boxing insights, but he was destined to enrich his martial arts by contacts made through his work.

When Xiong was 23 years old, he began a career in the military, which dealt with security and military operations. At 29, he was Adjunct Director of the Anhui Province government office, and at 35 he went on to a management position in the Funing County garrisons. During this period, Xiong met Old Frame Yang Style Taijiquan master Hu Puan (1878-1947), who became his most influential teacher. Hu's nickname was "Hu Hu," meaning "Tiger Hu."

Hu was born in Anhui Province, Jing County. He served as the Department Chief of Jiangsu Province Civil Administration. As a sinologist well-known for his books and poetry, Hu taught at Shanghai University. While in Shanghai, he had an opportunity to meet and study with a number of high caliber taiji masters. He practiced daily starting at 6:00am for over 18 years, until he became disabled by a stroke and resulting paralysis.[1]

Who was Hu's primary taiji teacher? Sources differ, stating he studied with:

1) Chen Weiming (1881-1958) [2]
2) Yang Jianhou (1839-1917) [3]
3) Yang Chengfu (1883-1936) [4]
4) Yang Shaohou (1862-1930) [5]
5) Le Huanzhi (1899-1960) [6]

At his desk, Hu Puan (1878-1947) was famed as a China scholar and taijiquan master. *www.taiji.net.cn*

Most statements regarding Hu Puan's teachers simply say that he studied with this particular person or that one. Furthermore, there are questions about the length of time that Hu studied with his teachers. What could he have learned from them? One reference says "Yang Chengfu and disciple Mr. Hu Puan ... compared notes together, making a thorough study of taijiquan, gaining thorough and penetrating insights into taiji gongfu."[7] To state that Hu was Yang Chengfu's "disciple" is a strong statement. Unfortunately, I have not found solid evidence to substantiate this pronouncement.

Hu Puan probably met all of these teachers and may have studied with each to different degrees. But it is interesting to note that he spoke so highly of Le Huanzhi (1899-1960), who was from Gushi County in Henan. Le was a medical doctor and also a senior disciple of Dong Yingjie (1898-1961). In his published memoir, Hu wrote that Le's taijiquan is extremely fine. Hu wrote that—from his own push hands experience with Yang Chengfu, Sun Lutang, Wu Jianquan, and Le Huanzhi—Le proved superior, and his touch was highly effective yet had an undetectable source, "like passing clouds and flowing water," "as not having matter."[8]

Because the sources are obscure, it is difficult to know from whom Hu Puan received his taijiquan instruction. Also, the lineage for Xiong has not been evenly defined. There are a few sources that state that Xiong was a disciple of Yang Shaohou.[9] This seems to be an assumption based primarily on what

Xiong taught. However, both Xiong and Hu Puan probably had some contact with Yang Shaohou. What we do know for sure is that, in his autobiography (1962), Xiong himself only mentions Hu Puan in regards to the transmission of the Yang Style Old Frame. This does not negate the possibility that Xiong met other Yang Style Taiji masters, or learned their methods via Hu Puan.

Xiong may have "studied thoroughly with Hu Puan," but he no doubt did have good relations with other taijiquan masters.[10] One source states that Xiong had the chance to meet Yang Jianhou while staying in Beijing for official business. It gave him the opportunity to seek advice about taijiquan, especially regarding the two-person routine call *sanshou* ("dispersing hands"). At this time, Xiong studied wholeheartedly and was able to grasp the deeper mysteries of the art.[11] Yet another source mentions that Yang Jianhou taught in Funing County, and Xiong sought his advice for the sanshou practice.[12] Liang Dongcai (aka, T. T. Liang) states that Yang Jianhou taught Xiong sanshou. Liang also maintains that nobody could have possibly learned it from Yang Chengfu, because his father Yang Jianhou died before he could teach it to him (Hayward, 2000: 61).

Since Xiong had to take part in policy discussions falling within the range of his official military duties, he had a great opportunity to meet many people who were highly skilled in a variety of martial traditions. They could compare their studies and benefit by observing the full scope of Chinese martial arts. Over the decades, Xiong received a solid grounding in Northern and Southern Shaolin and taijiquan from his personal teachers and from contact with others through his military career. Here are some highlights from his career:[13]

Age	Position
39	Regimental Commander, Revolutionary Army
40	Jiangsu Province Funing County Public Security Bureau Chief, and concurrent position as Production Brigade Chief
49	Jiangsu Province Funing County Magistrate
52	Security Major General Brigade Commander
53	Security Assistant Commandant
54	Security Major General Commander
58	Major General Group Commander
60	Deputy Commanding Officer, Military Headquarters

In 1949, the Nationalist Party under Chiang Kai-shek retreated to Taiwan, and the Communist Party established the People's Republic of China (PRC) on the mainland. Xiong resigned and moved to Taiwan when "nearly 600,000 Nationalist troops and their dependents withdrew from the mainland to Taiwan."[14] It is commonly said that part of this migratory wave included four famed "Big Dogs" of taijiquan: Zheng Manqing (1901-1975), Guo Lianying,

Shi Diaomei and Xiong Yanghe.

After settling in Yilan city in 1953, Xiong tirelessly taught taiji. Eventually, Xiong Style practitioners came to number over 10,000. Xiong's most significant contribution to taiji's legacy is the through preservation and transmission of Yang Taijiquan as a fighting art and exercise system, most notably being the two-person practice of *sanshou*. In addition, his books leave a detailed record of the system.

Even in his twilight years, Xiong was up daily at 4:30 am to start his day, which included his regular taiji classes. In addition to chanting Buddhist scriptures, practicing brush calligraphy, and reading military history, he wrote books, which leave a detailed record of the taiji system for following generations. He was a Buddhist who treated his disciples with a fatherly affection. He died on October 29, 1981 in Yilan Yuan Shan Rongmin Hospital at the age of 94.

Left: Master Guo Tingxian (1923-2002) was one of Xiong Yanghe's top disciples, and the teacher of Lin Jianhong. *Photograph courtesy of Lin Jianhong.*
Right: Master Yang Qingyu (1915-2002) was one of Xiong Yanghe's longtime students and close confidant. Born in Henan, he served in the military and moved to Taiwan. *Photograph by M. DeMarco.*

Xiong Yanghe's Curriculum as Presented by Lin Jianhong

On the *Neijia Formosa* website, David Chesser writes this regarding Xiong's curriculum: "This amount of training makes it the most complete version of taiji practiced on the island. I simply haven't found anything that compares to it."[15] In order to present some of Xiong Yanghe's system in this anthology, photographs were provided by Robert Yu, who contacted Master Lin Jianhong during a visit to Taiwan in October of 2006.

Master Lin Jianhong studied under Guo Tingxian, a top Xiong Yanghe disciple. Through Guo, Lin also learned Hua Tuo's Five Animal Frolics. Lin teaches in the Taipei area, including Liberty Square (formerly called the Chiang Kai-shek Memorial Square). Mr. Robert Yu visited Master Lin's class three times, saying that Lin and his students were refreshing to meet, "open, friendly and competent" people (R. Yu, personal communication, November 3, 2006). Yu provided over 100 photographs and reference materials for this article. Now in his mid-50s, Master Lin enjoys teaching, usually with the help of his assistant Ms. Ye Jinxiu, as shown on the following pages.

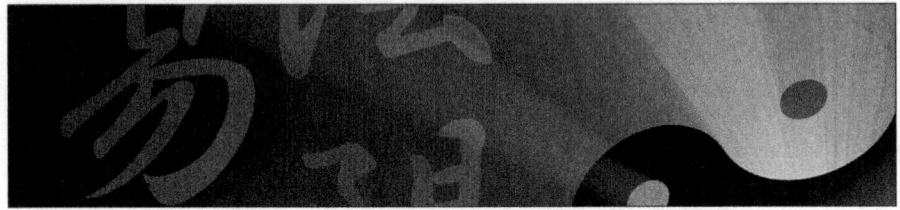

Courtesy of iStockphoto.com.

Xiong Style Curriculum

- Yang Family Old Frame Xiong Style Taijiquan (111 style) 楊家老架熊氏太極拳
- Taiji Basic (standing) Post 太極基本樁
- Taiji Qigong 太極氣功
- Push hands (tuishou) 推手
- Dispersing Hands (sanshou) 散手
- Taiji sword 太極劍
- knife 刀
- stick 棍
- staff 桿
- paired swords (two-person) 對劍
- paired knives (two-person) 對刀
- paired sticks (two-person) 對桿
- paired staves (two-person) 對棍
- Six Directions Flower Spear (Liulu Huaqiang) 六路花槍
- Spring and Autumn broadsword 春秋大刀
- double swords 雙劍
- Mizong Boxing 秘宗拳 【迷蹤拳】
- Four Gates Hong Boxing 四門洪拳
- Young Hong Boxing 小洪拳
- Sunlight Palm (Ziyang Zhang Deng) 曦陽掌等
- and more

Lin Jianhong

Long Form Solo Routine

Selected postures from the traditional long routine consisting of 111 postures.

1) Beginning posture 2) Ward-off left

3) Ward-off right 4) Rollback

5) Press 6) Double Elbow

7) Single Whip 8) Raise Hands

9) Rooster Stands on One Leg 10) Snake Creeps Down

11) Ride Tiger

12) Bend Bow Shoot Tiger

Five Animal Frolics

A superb way to cultivate taijiquan principles is to devote a few minutes a day to these exercises. Master Lin was fortunate to learn this system from Guo Tingxian. Mr. Lin's student, Ms. Ye Jinxiu, leads the group.

Long Form Solo Routine Group Practice

Long Form
Solo Routine Group Practice

Mr. Lin closely observes each student during practice sessions and later suggests ways to improve their practice.

Master Lin teaches a variety of students at different locations and class times. Most want to learn taiji for health purposes and the good comradery. Others, usually younger students, delve into the fighting traditions. Regardless, if you study Xiong Style, you will get a mixture of both due to the completeness of this traditional system.

Staff

Broadsword

Sanshou

"Dispersing Hands" is a two-person routine designed to give advanced students a realistic feel for taiji as a combative art. It can be practiced at various speeds and includes functions from the solo form as well as others derived from Chen Family Style. It seems Grandmaster Xiong learned this from Hu Puan, but there is probably a link to Yang Jianhou as well. Contact is never broken during sanshou practice.

Concluding Remarks on Xiong Style Taijiquan

Like the story of the blind men examining an elephant, this chapter can only represent the author's personal findings limited by a relative lack of reference materials, the difficulty in translating Chinese texts accurately, and time available for research. I take responsibility for any shortcomings and welcome any helpful feedback. Hopefully, despite such limitations, the material presented here can broaden the perspective on taijiquan, considering the historical setting where the art was developed by the leading Yang Family lineage representatives.

We have found that there were two major factors influencing early Yang Style development. The first is the nearly incomprehensible violence from the downfall of the Qing Dynasty to the founding of the Peoples' Republic of China, especially during the Republican Period (1911-1949) that soaked the Chinese soil with blood when disorder was at a maximum. It was a time when many sought out superior fighting methods and practiced as if their lives depended upon it. It is no surprise that taijiquan was a desirable system to learn and that it migrated from a small village to be practiced by bodyguards in major cities where military and security personnel were found.

The other major factor influencing taiji's history stems from the exhaustion felt by the country and its population after centuries of rebellions and foreign interventions. Years of struggle, defeat, and humiliation inspired a growing sense of nationalism and an era of "self-strengthening" for the country. One way to cure the "sick man of Asia" was to spread taiji for health: it was found to be highly effective as a form of exercise, no special gear or facility was required, and it was inexpensive when practiced in groups. Millions are healthier because of it.

If we keep in mind the two influences mentioned above while looking at the early Yang Style lineage, a special interrelationship unfolds between taiji and Chinese social history. Between the birth of Yang Luchan and the death of Xiong Yanghe, factions of China's population fought for survival for 150 years before finally emerging as a nation at peace. No doubt Yang Luchan's taiji was a fighting art, but what did it look like? How did he practice? What was the depth of his knowledge?

Most taiji styles today have evolved away from their martial roots. This evolution paralleled the decline of violence in China and the growing social and political stability. At its highest levels, taiji as a fighting art has always been transmitted to a relatively small number of people. Teaching *en masse* for public health has reached millions. As a result, a vast majority of taiji practitioners know form, but little of function. The reasons one has for learning taiji affects how the form is practiced and looks. We cannot see how Yang Luchan practiced, but the system preserved by Xiong Yanghe seems to be a good indicator and is valued for preserving a great tradition on Taiwan that was nearly lost during the Communist Cultural Revolution (1966-1976), a social movement that included a crusade to rid China of "old ways of thinking," such as those exhibited in the traditional martial arts.

Xiong Style offers combative elements that were necessary during the extreme chaos found in China during the early Yang Family transmissions of the art. Yang Luchan studied Chen Style and aspects of this are reflected in Xiong Style too: stances are often low and wide, applications are effective, training methods in push-hands and sanshou are practical, and the inclusion of weaponry is encompassing. Even though Xiong's system retains the old Yang flavor, he lived forty years longer than Yang Chengfu, and into the post-1949 era. He was motivated to teach for two reasons. He taught close students taiji as a fighting art and as an exercise for health and longevity. Thousands of other students were taught basically for "self-strengthening."

This brief overview of Xiong Style helps define and give meaning to the words "taijiquan." Taiji is not just an exercise and not only a fighting art. It is both, and its dual nature is inherent in the teachings of true masters. One who has mastered Xiong's system, or the early Yang Family systems, can impart the theory and knowledge applicable in both areas as a combative art and exercise system. The mix is largely determined by the teacher-student relationship and the motives involved. Yang Family Xiong Style Taijiquan gives us an unique opportunity to look back in time when the template of Yang Style was forged. As the system thrives in Taiwan under Xiong's disciples and their own disciples—teachers such as Lin Jianhong and Lin Chaolai—we see that the old system has been preserved, while even spreading outside Taiwan to benefit others. It's a taste of "old wine in a new bottle."

Acknowledgements

The impetus for this article came from Mr. Robert Lin-I Yu, a noted baguazhang and xingyi instructor (disciple of Hong Yixiang, Zhou Jincai, and others in Taiwan). From his home in Madison, Wisconsin, Yu called to say he would be returning to Taiwan in October (2006) to conduct martial arts research and visit relatives. "Would you like me to do anything for you while there?" My only response was that, if he wished, he could contact Mr. Lin Shengxuan (one of my Xiong Style Taiji classmates) and any other Xiong Style instructor he could find. He followed up and returned to the U.S. with a huge stack of photographs, notes, copies of hand written documents, books, and unpublished manuscripts from Xiong Style instructors. A special thanks to these two fine gentlemen for the friendship and support, and to Master Lin Jianghong, Ms. Ye Jinxiu, and fellow students for kindly participating.

Robert Yu and Lin Shengxuan
in 228 Memorial Park.

Short List of Xiong Students

Cao Zenghua	曹增華	Lin Xianghua	林祥華
Chen Deyang	陳德洋	Lu Yuxuan	陸雨軒
Chen Huang	陳皇	Lü Zhenzhong	呂振忠
Chen Xiaoyin	陳曉寅	Meng Shanfu	孟善夫
Chen Xinggui	陳興桂	Qiu Shuzhou	裘署舟
Chen Zhenhe	陳珍和	Rao Shunchen	饒舜臣
Guo Tingxian	郭廷獻	Yang Qingyu	楊清玉
Huang Guozhi	黃國治	Ye Shiyi	葉式意
Huang Qinglin	黃清麟	Yu Xianquan	俞賢詮
Jan Tiangong	天拱	Wan Xiaoyan	萬小燕
Li Guoguang	李國光	Wang Jingzhi	王靜之
Li Rixin	李日新	Wang Juemin	王覺民
Lin Chaolai	林朝來	Wei Guang	魏廣
Lin Lianfu	林連富	Zhang Nan	張楠
Lin Lianzhi	林連袄	Zhang Zhongping	張仲平
Lin Qingzhi	林清智	Zou Xueyuan	鄒學元

Other Xiong Students

Liang Dongcai (Liang Tsung Tsai)	梁棟材
Liu Chenhuan (Abraham Liu)	
Tao Bingxiang (Tao Ping-Siang)	陶怲祥
Zhong Dazhen (Tchoung Ta-tchen)	鍾大振

People Mentioned in the Article

Chen Changxing	陳長興	Sun Lutang	孫祿堂
Chen Yanxi	陳延熙	Tang Dianqing	唐殿卿
Chen Weiming	陳微明	Wu Jianquan	吳鑑泉
Dong Yingjie	董英杰	Yang Banhou	楊班侯
Du Yuze	杜毓澤	Yang Chengfu	楊澄甫
Gan Fengchi	甘鳳池	Yang Jianhou	楊健侯
Guo Lianying	郭連英	Yang Luchan	楊露禪
Hu Puan	胡扑安	Yang Qingyu	楊清玉
Le Huanzhi	乐奂之	Yang Shaohou	楊少侯
Lin Jianhong	林建宏	Yin Wanbang	殷萬邦
Lin Shengxuan	林聖軒	Xiong Weizhen	熊渭珍
Liu He	劉和	Xiong Yanghe	熊養和
Liu Zhongfang	劉仲仿	Zheng Manqing	鄭曼青
Shi Diaomei	施調梅		

Places

Anhui Province	安徽省	Henan Province	河南省
Chen Village	陳家溝	Jiangsu Province	江蘇省
Funing County	阜寧縣	Jing County	经县
Guangping County	廣平縣	Yilan County	宜蘭縣
Gushi County	固始县	Yongnian County	永年县
Hebei Province	河北省		

References for Website Sources

1. http://yuehuanzhi.blog.sohu.com
2. www.taiji.net.cn/liu/wlys/200712/6426.shtml; http://yuehuanzhi.blog.sohu.com
3. http://blog.udn.com/article/trackback.jsp?uid=wang6196192001&aid=107787
4. http://tw.myblog.yahoo.com/q3taichi/article?mid=23&sc=1
5. http://library.taiwanschoolnet.org; http://blog.youthwant.com.tw/vadjra/vadjra/ 6395839/
6. http://yuehuanzhi.blog.sohu.com; www.xici.net/u6819319/d19792891.htm
7. http://tw.myblog.yahoo.com/q3taichi/profile
8. www.xici.net/u6819319/d19792891.htm
9. www.dotaichi.com
10. http://blog.sina.com.tw/lkk_blog/article.php?pbgid=36074&entryid=320007
11. http://www.lin-gi.com.tw/discuss/Viewtopic.asp? Subject ID=7135&Sign=150
12. http://tw.myblog.yahoo.com/jin_cang/article?mid=1003&prev=2170 &next= 554& =f&fid=3

[13] http://blog.udn.com/wang6196192001/1067085
[14] http://taiwanreview.nat.gov.tw/fp.asp?xItem=589&CtNode=128
[15] http://chessman71.wordpress.com/2006/05/15/yang-shao-hous-taiji/)

References – Chinese

Anonymous, (1987). *Mr. Xiong's 100th birthday commemorative special edition.* (n.p.).

Anonymous, (1984). *National arts master Xiong Yanghe commemorative collection.* (n.p.).

Lin, Caolai (2007). *Yang family old frame Xiong style taijiquan.* DVD. Yilan, Taiwan: Chin-yu Martial Art Study Association.

Yang, Qingyu (1976). *Xiong style taijiquan long form, push-hands, and sword form.* Private film collection.

Yang, Qingyu (1988). *Autobiography.* Self published.

Yang, Qingyu (n.d.). *A brief biography of Xiong Yanghe.* Self published.

Xiong, Y.H. (1962). *Autobiography.* Self published.

Xiong, Y.H. (1963). *The taijiquan explained.* Taipei: Taiwan China Book Printing House.

Xiong, Y.H. (1971). *Taiji swordsmanship illustrated.* Yilan, Taiwan: Lu Feng Printing and Publishing House.

Xiong, Y.H. (1975). *The taijiquan explained.* 3rd edition. Taipei: Huge Distribution Planning Company.

References – English

Hucker, C. (1975). *China's imperial past: An introduction to Chinese history and culture.* Stanford, CA: Stanford University Press.

DeMarco, M. (1992). The origin and evolution of taijiquan. *Journal of Asian Martial Arts,* 1(1): 8-25.

Gallagher, P. (2007). *Drawing silk: Masters' secrets for successful tai chi practice.* Charleston, SC: BookSurge.

Hayward, R. (2000). *T'ai-chi ch'uan: Lessons with master T.T. Liang.* St. Paul, MN: Shu-Kuang Press.

Kuhn, P. (1970). *Rebellion and Its Enemies in Late Imperial China: Militarization and Social Structure, 1796~1864.* Cambridge, MA: Harvard University Press.

Kurland, H. (May 1998). "Hsiung Yang-Ho's san shou form." *T'ai chi Ch'uan and Wellness Newsletter.* Downloaded July 16, 2009.

Kurland, H. (2003). "History of a rare t'ai-chi form: San shou." http://www.selfgrowth.com/articles/Kurland3.html. Downloaded July 16, 2009.

Lu, S. (Yun, Z., Trans.) (2006). *Combat techniques of taiji, xingyi, and bagua.* Berkeley, CA: Blue Snake Books.

Olson, S. (1999). *T'ai chi thirteen sword: A sword master's manual.* Burbank, CA: Multi-Media Books.

Olson, S. (1999). *T'ai chi sensing-hands: A complete guide to t'ai chi t'ui-shou training from original Yang Family records.* Burbank, CA: Multi-Media Books.

Olson, S. (1992). *The teachings of master T.T. Liang: Imagination becomes reality, the complete guide to the 150 posture solo form.* St. Paul, MN: Dragon Door Publications.

Russell, J. (2004). *The tai chi two-person dance: Tai chi with a partner.* Berkeley, CA: North Atlantic Books.

Sheridan, J. (1977). *China in Disintegration: The Republican Era in Chinese history 1912-1949.* New York: The Free Press.

Schurmann, F. and Schell, O. (1967). *Republican China: Nationalism, war, and the rise of Communism 1911-1949.* New York: Vintage Book.

Wakeman, F. (1977). *The fall of imperial China.* New York: The Free Press.

Wile, D. (1996). *T'ai-chi touchstones: Yang family secret transmissions.* Brooklyn, NY: Sweet Chi Press.

Xiong Yanghe Photographs

As part of its goal to maintain cultural records, Taiwan's National Digital Archives Program (see www.ndap.org.tw) has digital photographs of Xiong Yanghe in the collection which can be viewed in thumbnail and large format (view at http:/ digitalarchives.tw).

index

Anglo-Chinese War, 47
baguazhang, 4, 23-25, 29, 36, 48, 65
bajiquan, 23
Beijing, 1-2, 24, 45, 48, 50, 54
Beijing Physical Culture Research Institute, 45
Boxer Uprising, 48
Chan Hak Fu, 21 note 4
Chen Changxing, 2, 45-46, 50, 67
Chen Gengyun, 50, 54
Chen Village, 1, 7, 45-46, 50, 67
Chen Weiming, 53, 67
Chen Yenxi, 50
Cheng Tinghua, 23, 29
Chiang Kai-shek, 49, 54, 56
Chinese wrestling, 23, 29
Communist Party, 21 note 3, 49, 54, 65
Deng, Huijian, 17, 20
dispersing hands (sanshou), 54-56, 63, 65
Dong Haichuan, 4, 9
Dong Yingjie, 53, 67
Du Yuzi, 50
Dun Prince Palace, 4
eight doors, 6
Eight Harmonies Boxing, 52
eight techniques, 5-7
Feng Yuxiang (General), 48
Five Animal Frolics, 56, 60
five steps, 5-7
four corners, 26
four directions, 25
Four Important Points of Solo Practice, 5
Fu Zhongquan, 2, 9, 10 note 5
Gan Fengchi, 52, 67
Guo Lianying, 54, 67
Guo Shaojiong, 13, 20
Guo Tingxian, 55-56, 60, 66

Guo Yunshen, 23
Hao Weizhen, 24-25
Henan 64 Form, 5-7, 9
Hong Kong, 11-15, 17-18, 21 note 1
Hong Kong Jin Wu Sports Association, 21
Hong Kong Taiji Main Association, 21
Hong Kong YMCA, 12
Hu Puan, 52-54, 63, 67
Huang Feihong, 12, 20
Jianquan Taiji Association, 13-14
Le Huanzhi, 53, 67
Li Jiying, 3
Li Kuiyuan, 23
Li Ruidong, 2-7, 9
Liang Dongcai, 54
Lin Chaola, 65-66
Ling Shan, 2, 9
Liu He, 51, 67
local defense, 46, 50
Lu Botang, 14, 18-20
Ma Jiangxiong, 15
Ma Yueliang, 15, 20
Mongkok School, 18, 21 notes 1 and 2
Nationalist Party, 49, 51, 54
Opium War, 47
platforms competition (leitai), 52
push hands, 7, 17-18, 24, 53, 56, 65
Shanghai, 12-15, 45, 52
Shaolinquan, 23, 45, 48, 51-52, 54
Shen Xianglin, 13, 20
Shi Diaomei, 55, 67
Sino-French War, 47
Sino-Japanese War, 47
Singapore, 14
South China Sports Association, 12
Sun Jianyun, 22, 24, 27
Taiping Rebellion, 47

Tang Dianqing, 52
thirteen postures, 24-25
Three Important Points on Partner
    Practice, 6
Three Powers Posture (santi), 27-28
Twelve Continuous Fists, 4
Wan Chun, 2, 9
Wanchai District, 12-13, 21 note 2
Wang Lanting, 2-4, 9
Warlord Period, 11, 48-49
White Crane, 21 note 4
White Lotus Society, 47
Wu-Chan fight, 14
Wu Chaojie, 17, 20
Wu Dakui, 12-15, 17-18, 20, 21 note 2
Wu Daqi, 13, 17, 20
Wu Gongyi, 11-14, 17-20, 21 note 4
Wu Gongzao, 11, 14-17, 20, 21 note 3
Wu Jianquan, 10 notes 2 and 8, 11-15,
    17-18, 20, 21 notes 1 and 4, 53
Wu Kangnian, 14, 17, 20
Wu Quanyou, 2, 9, 17
Wu Ruqing, 1, 9
Wu Tunan, 1-2, 9
Steel, Kelvin, 17
Wu Yanxia, 13, 17, 20
Wu Yinghua, 15, 20
Wu Yuxiang, 9, 10 note 1, 24
Wu Wenbiao, 17, 20
Wuqing Taijiquan, 3-4
Xiao Huilong, 18
xingyiquan, 23-25, 27, 29, 65
xinyiquan, 4, 9
Yang Banhou, 2, 4, 9, 45-46, 50-51
Yang Chengfu, 45-46, 50-51, 53-54, 65
Yang Jianhou, 45-46, 51, 53-54, 63
Yang Luchan, 1-5, 7, 9, 10 note 4, 43, 45-46,
    50-51, 64-65
Yang Qingyu, 55, 66
Yang Shaohou, 45-46, 50-51, 53-54
Ye Shuliang, 18-20
Yin Wanbang, 52
Yip Man, 12, 20
Yongnian, 1, 9, 10 note 1, 45
Yuan Shikai, 50
Zhang Fengqi, 2, 9
Zhang Shaotang, 1
Zhang Wansheng, 4
Zheng Manqing, 54
Zhong Yueping, 13-14, 20, 21 note 1

Printed in Great Britain
by Amazon

63150142R00047